GIVING THANKS

HOME TO HEATHER CREEK

GIVING THANKS

Kristin Eckhardt

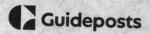

Home to Heather Creek is a trademark of Guideposts.

Copyright © 2023 by Guideposts. All rights reserved.

This book, or parts thereof, may not be reproduced, stored in a retrieval system, or transmitted in any form or by any means, electronic, mechanical, photocopying, recording, or otherwise, without the written permission of the publisher.

The characters and events in this book are fictional, and any resemblance to actual persons or events is coincidental.

Scripture references are from the following sources: *The Holy Bible, King James Version* (KJV). *The Holy Bible, New International Version* (NIV). Copyright © 1973, 1978, 1984, 2011 by Biblica, Inc. Used by permission of Zondervan. All rights reserved worldwide. www.zondervan.com

Published by Guideposts Books & Inspirational Media
100 Reserve Road, Suite E200
Danbury, CT 06810
Guideposts.org

Cover by Lookout Design, Inc.
Interior design by Cindy LaBreacht
Additional design work by Müllerhaus
Typeset by Aptara, Inc.

ISBN 978-1-959634-63-8 (hardcover)
ISBN 978-1-959634-65-2 (epub)
ISBN 978-1-959634-64-5 (epdf)

Printed in the United States of America
10 9 8 7 6 5 4

Acknowledgments

In memory of my mother-in-law, Beverly Eckhardt, who gave me her wonderful son and her delicious Date Cake recipe.

—Kristin Eckhardt

Home to Heather Creek

Before the Dawn

Sweet September

Circle of Grace

Homespun Harvest

A Patchwork Christmas

An Abundance of Blessings

Every Sunrise

Promise of Spring

April's Hope

Seeds of Faith

On the Right Path

Sunflower Serenade

Second Chances

Prayers and Promises

Giving Thanks

GIVING THANKS

Chapter One

"And now, ladies, I'm going to show you the secret ingredient to making the perfect appliqués for your quilts."

Charlotte sat at a row of tables in Fabrics and Fun with six other women who had signed up for Rosemary's Friday afternoon quilting class. She watched her sister-in-law reach into the wicker basket next to her and pull out a roll of freezer paper.

Julia Benson, seated at the table next to Charlotte, laughed. "Freezer paper? Is this a quilting class or a cooking class?"

Rosemary laughed with her. "Charlotte's the cook in our family. But the freezer paper is part of a technique that makes appliqué both easy and fun."

Charlotte smiled at the compliment about her cooking skills as she began to lay out the quilt blocks on the table. Every member of the class had pieced simple nine-patch blocks, and now they were learning the technique of appliquéing over the pieced block.

She looked around the tables, amazed that the same quilt pattern could look so different just by the variety of colors and fabrics selected.

"Now here's how it works," Rosemary began, cutting off a small section of freezer paper from the roll. "The first step is to trace the shape of the appliqué onto the dull side of the paper. That's very important for later on."

Charlotte watched her trace a heart onto the freezer paper with a pencil. "Do we need to make room for the seam allowance when we trace?"

"No, we'll do that when we cut out the fabric." Rosemary used her scissors to quickly cut out the heart she'd just traced onto the freezer paper.

"Now comes the fun part," Rosemary continued. "Using an iron, gently press the shiny side of the freezer-paper cutout onto the *wrong* side of the fabric that you want to use for the appliqué."

Everyone watched in silence as Rosemary pressed the warm iron on top of the paper heart, fusing it to the red cotton fabric underneath.

"And there you have it." Rosemary held up the appliqué. "The shiny surface of the freezer paper adheres to the fabric. Now all you have to do is trim around the excess fabric, leaving a three-eighths-inch seam allowance around the paper pattern. Simply press the seam allowance around the freezer-paper template to create a smooth crease. Then you're ready to tear away the freezer paper and sew the appliqué to your quilt block."

"That *is* easy," Julia exclaimed.

Charlotte raised her hand in the air. "What is the iron setting?"

"Good question," Amanda Hostetler chimed in from the next table.

"It will depend on the fabric you're using," Rosemary

replied. "If it's cotton, then set your iron on the cotton setting. For a more delicate fabric, like satin, you'll need to use a cooler setting."

Rosemary tore off several pieces of freezer paper and passed them around to the class members. "Now I'd like each of you to try it. I've got a basket of templates on each table, along with some remnant cotton fabric so you can practice."

Charlotte waited until Julia fished a heart template and a piece of pink fabric out of the basket. Then she selected a duck template and a handkerchief-sized square of orange fabric for herself.

Julia leaned over to look at her handiwork. "I like the combination of colors you chose for the baby quilt, especially the blues, greens, and purples.

"Thank you." Charlotte reached out to pull a loose thread off one of the blocks. "Bill and Anna made it easier for me to select the colors when they decided to find out ahead of time if they're having a boy or a girl."

"And . . . ?" Julia prodded.

"And I can't wait to meet my new grandson," Charlotte said with a wide smile.

"So they're having a boy," Julia cried. "Oh, how exciting! Isn't technology something?"

Amanda chuckled beside them. "Just don't count on technology too much. My great-niece had a frilly pink nursery all ready for her baby after the doctor told her it was going to be a girl. They certainly got a big surprise when the baby was born."

"Oh, my," Charlotte said. "A boy instead of a girl?"

Amanda nodded. "Good thing the first name they picked out could work for either sex. Instead of Taylor Marie

Callahan, the baby's name is Taylor Charles Callahan. He is a little cutie, though. I don't think they mind a bit that they got a different baby than what they were expecting."

Charlotte wouldn't mind either. She knew that God didn't make mistakes, even if technology occasionally did. Still, she hoped technology was right this time because Bill had his heart set on having a boy.

As she traced the duck onto the freezer paper, she wondered if Pete and Dana planned to have children. She hoped so. Just the thought of a new baby living at Heather Creek Farm made her smile.

"Look how far you've come with your quilt," Rosemary said as she walked up to Charlotte's table. "You must be so excited about your new grandbaby."

"I am," Charlotte agreed. "December is right around the corner, so I'll have just enough time to get this quilt done before the baby arrives. I can't think of a nicer Christmas present than another grandchild."

Some people might think she had her hands full with the three grandchildren she was raising at home, two of them teenagers. But Charlotte knew a grandmother could never run short of love.

"Sounds like you'll be keeping busy," Amanda said. "Does that mean you won't be selling any of your pies this year? I have my entire family coming for Thanksgiving, and I was hoping to buy a few of your delicious pies to serve for dessert."

"Sorry," Charlotte replied. "I'm out of the pie-making business."

She remembered how hectic her life had become last year when she'd formed the Heather Creek Pie Company to sell her popular homemade pies for the Thanksgiving holiday.

Her grandchildren had pitched in, and even though the experience had helped them all grow closer, she didn't ever want to put herself under that much pressure again.

This year, Charlotte was looking forward to a relaxing Thanksgiving at home with Bob, Pete, and the grandchildren. Bill and his family would be there too, along with Pete's fiancée, Dana, and her parents.

It pleased Charlotte that she actually had time to plan a nice dinner. Last year she'd been so busy with her pie business that she could barely keep up with her daily tasks. This year promised to be more relaxing. The soybeans had all been cut, and the corn harvest was nearly done. The kids seemed happy and were all busy with their school activities.

Best of all, a new baby boy Stevenson would be arriving for Christmas.

As she practiced the freezer-paper technique, Charlotte thought about how quickly time moved. It seemed like just yesterday that Denise had shared the news that she was expecting her first baby.

Now Sam would be graduating from Bedford High in a few months and then heading off to college. Emily wouldn't be far behind him, leaving Christopher alone with his grandparents as he entered his teenage years.

There was no use in contemplating all the changes the future held.

Living for today brought the most joy and the most reward. That's a lesson she wanted to teach all her grandchildren, including the one who would soon be wrapped in this baby quilt.

Charlotte couldn't wait to meet him.

Chapter Two

"This is cool," said the new boy sitting across the desk from Christopher.

His name was Wyatt Carpenter and he'd recently moved to Bedford. Christopher didn't know much about him, but the kid had latched on to him and Dylan at recess two days ago and made their usual twosome a threesome.

Wyatt had short blond hair, a short body, and short pant legs that hung between his ankles and his knees. He was a misfit, which meant he fit in with Dylan and Christopher just fine.

Their teacher, Miss Luka, must have noticed their friendship, because she'd paired Wyatt with Christopher for science class. They were supposed to be doing research for a report about an invention and were looking for ideas in *Current Science* magazine.

The door to the classroom opened and Dylan Lonetree walked inside. He'd been in the nurse's office with a headache.

"How are you feeling, Dylan?" Miss Luka asked him.

"Better, I guess," he replied, one shoulder moving in a twisted shrug.

The teacher smiled at him. "I'm glad to hear it. Everyone is paired up for their science reports already, so why don't you join Christopher and Wyatt's team?"

Dylan brightened as he headed toward them, grabbed a chair and placed it next to Wyatt. "Have you picked an invention yet?"

"Not yet," Christopher told him. "It's hard to decide, 'cause there are so many good ones."

The boys paged through the magazine, finding it hard to pass up stories like the one about tiny insects that could live in your nose.

"How about this one?" Dylan said at last, tapping his index finger against a page headlined, BENJAMIN FRANKLIN INVENTED THE LIGHTNING ROD.

"What exactly does a lightning rod do?" Christopher asked.

"I know the answer," Wyatt said excitedly. "You put a lightning rod on your roof so it doesn't electrocute your house."

"I've never heard of an electrocuted house," Christopher said skeptically.

"Well, how about an electrocuted barn?" Wyatt countered. "On my uncle's farm, there was a pig that *died* because it was leaning against a metal fence when lightning struck a tree nearby."

Dylan's brow crinkled. "Why did the pig die if the lightning struck a tree?"

"Because electricity can travel under the ground," Wyatt said. "My dad warned me never to lean against a fence in a rainstorm. The metal posts are buried in the ground and electricity can travel underground up to two miles."

Christopher whistled low. "That's a long way."

"It's also really cool," Dylan said. "Let's do our report on the invention of the lightning rod."

"Sounds good to me," Wyatt agreed.

"Me too," Christopher said. Then he got a great idea: "Maybe we can even make a real lightning rod as a visual aid when we present the report to the class."

Christopher knew Miss Luka was really big on visual aids.

"Cool!" Wyatt exclaimed.

"But how do we make one?" Dylan asked.

Christopher looked over at the computer station at the back of the classroom and saw that one of the computers was free.

"Come on," he told his research partners. "Let's look on the internet. I bet we can find directions on how to build one.

It took them only ten minutes to find a website with blueprints for building their own lightning rods, along with a list of materials they'd need.

Christopher printed off a copy of the information just as Miss Luka announced that science time was over. He looked at the clock, noting that the school day would end in less than half an hour.

"We've had some people struggling with fractions lately," Miss Luka told the class. "So let's use this next twenty minutes or so to get a good head start on your math homework for tomorrow."

Christopher never had any trouble with math and had finished all of the homework problems at the end of the math lesson. That meant he could spend the time designing the lightning rod. Miss Luka usually didn't care what students chose to work on during study time as long as they were quiet.

He pulled a spiral notebook out of his desk and opened it to the first page, where he began to copy down the materials he'd need to build the lightning rod.

Copper wire. Copper pipes. Aluminum brackets. As he wrote the words, Christopher wondered if he could find any of those things on the farm.

"Pssst," Dylan hissed beside him. "What's the answer to number ten?"

Christopher bit back a sigh as he turned to his friend. Normally, he didn't mind helping Dylan with math, but right now he wanted to study the blueprint for his lightning rod.

Dylan pushed his math paper closer to the edge of his desk so Christopher could have a better view. "I just don't get this one."

It took only a moment for Christopher to spot his mistake. "The denominators have to be equal before you can add them together."

"Oh, that's right." Dylan looked down at his paper and started to work on the problem.

Christopher turned back to his desk and took stock of the list on his paper. If he was good at making lightning rods, maybe he could start his own business, like Grandma had done with her pies last year. He could take orders or even sell them at AA Tractor Supply to earn some extra money.

He was tired of never having enough money to buy the things he wanted. It seemed like all the other kids at school had their own cell phones and computers.

Christopher would love to have a computer in his bedroom so he wouldn't have to share one with his brother and sister. Last night, he'd found a really cool website that had great stories about natural disasters. He had been right in the middle of a story about the 1906 San Francisco earthquake when Emily kicked him off the computer so she could do her homework.

He leaned over his desk, pencil in hand, as he began to slowly sketch a diagram of the kind of lightning rod he wanted to build. His tongue curled over his upper lip as he concentrated on making all of the lines as straight as possible.

He was barely aware of the other students in the classroom as he imagined showing off his completed lightning rod to his family. They'd all be so surprised that Christopher had built the lightning rod by himself. His grandpa would pat him on the shoulder and his grandma would give him a big hug.

"All right, class," Miss Luka announced. "The last bell is going to ring pretty soon so it's time to put your math homework in your backpacks if you haven't finished it."

She stood at the front of the classroom, her gaze moving across her students. "Everyone please clear off your desks as quickly as possible. I have a surprise for you before we leave today."

Intrigued, Christopher closed his notebook and stuffed it back inside his desk. Then he turned to Dylan. "What do you think it is?"

Dylan shrugged. "Maybe cookies?"

Christopher liked cookies as much as the next kid, but he'd eaten a big lunch so he wasn't all that hungry. He hoped the surprise was bigger than cookies. If he were a teacher, he'd surprise his students by giving them an extra recess every day or letting them play checkers all afternoon.

"Is everyone ready for the surprise?" Miss Luka asked the students, her eyes twinkling. "Raise your hand if you're ready."

Christopher's hand shot into the air as he leaned forward in anticipation. Dylan's waved wildly beside him, his body twisting and twitching with excitement. Wyatt had both hands in the air, which looked kind of silly to Christopher.

"Okay," Miss Luka said. "Now I want you to keep your hand up in the air *if* you can tell me the purpose of having a canned food drive."

Christopher slumped back in his chair, his raised arm growing rubbery with disappointment.

That was the surprise?

Cookies sounded better than a canned food drive. The school had held a canned food drive last year too. He'd brought a few cans of vegetables to donate just like everyone else.

Miss Luka pointed to a student in the front row. "Becca, why don't you tell us."

"A canned food drive is when you give your food to people who don't have any," Becca announced. "It makes everybody feel good."

Miss Luka nodded. "That's right. Our school is going to collect cans of food for the Adams County Food Pantry again this year. Our donations will help everyone in our community have a happy Thanksgiving."

"Is that the surprise?" Justin Taylor asked, sounding as disappointed as Christopher felt.

Miss Luka smiled. "Well, the surprise part is that we're doing it a little differently this year. The school is going to have a contest to see which class donates the most cans. The winning class will get to choose where they want to go on a field trip."

"We can go anywhere?" Tommy Fields blurted. "Like even Disneyland?"

The teacher's smile widened. "Anywhere within a sixty-mile radius of Bedford. That means a museum or a factory or even the television station in Harding. I'm sure we can think of lots of possibilities in this area."

Christopher's ears perked up when she mentioned the television station. He liked to watch the news with Grandpa, especially when the meteorologist came on with all his cool maps. He'd love to see all the machines they used to predict the weather.

"You can start bringing your cans on Monday," the teacher told the class. "The food drive will run for two weeks. We need to select a class leader who will encourage everyone to bring as many cans as possible and who will also keep track of how many cans the sixth grade class donates."

Several students raised their hand to volunteer, but Christopher held back. As much as he wanted to win the food drive and go on a field trip, he didn't want to be the one responsible in case his class lost the contest.

The teacher walked over to her desk and picked up the red-white-and-blue-sequined shoebox that held the names of every student in the class. "You guys know the drill. We're going to draw the name of our leader out of the box. I think that's the fairest way to do it."

Christopher sighed. Miss Luka was big on fairness. Every time there was a job to do, like cleaning the whiteboard or leading the class to the lunchroom, she drew a name out of the shoebox. Then, after a name was drawn, it would be set aside so that eventually every student in the class would be chosen to do something.

He held his breath as her hand dipped into the box then drew out a small card.

"And our wonderful canned food drive leader is . . ." Miss Luka paused to build the anticipation. "Christopher Slater!"

His classmates groaned, and Christopher felt a wave of heat in his cheeks. He didn't know if they were groaning because they were disappointed not to be chosen or because they thought he'd make a lousy leader.

Probably both.

"Christopher," Miss Luka said, "I'd like to speak to you after school today about your responsibilities as class leader. Will that work for you?"

He gave a silent nod, his gaze fixed on his desk.

"Lucky," a boy muttered behind him.

Christopher certainly didn't feel very lucky. He kept thinking about the contest and how much it would mean to his sixth-grade classmates to win. That was a lot of pressure. Especially when the prize was missing a whole day of school to go on a field trip.

When the last bell of the day finally rang, Christopher gathered his homework from his desk and placed it inside his backpack. For a moment, he thought about pretending he forgot about the meeting with the teacher and just walking out of the classroom.

But that would probably just get him into trouble.

Abandoning the idea, he slowly turned around and walked to Miss Luka's desk.

"I'm not sure I should be the leader of the canned food drive," Christopher said. "I've never done anything like that before."

"Oh, I'm sure you'll be excellent," Miss Luka replied, dismissing his doubts with a wave of her hand. "Now, what do you think is the best way to keep track of how many cans we donate compared to the rest of the school?"

Christopher thought about her question for a long moment. "We could do a graph or something."

She flashed a smile. "A graph is an excellent idea. If you draw it out on a poster board we can put it up on the wall so everyone can see how we're doing."

"You want *me* to draw it?" Christopher asked, reluctant to take any time away from his lightning rod project.

"You're the class leader." She studied him for a moment. "I'd also like you to talk to your classmates for the next few weeks and get some ideas for where they'd like to go for a field trip. Then if our class wins, we'll have a nice list of places to choose from."

Christopher nodded, intrigued by the idea that he could be in charge of helping decide where to go on a field trip. "I think the television station would be pretty cool."

"So do I. There are a lot of interesting places we could choose. I can't wait to hear all of the suggestions you get."

Christopher left the classroom feeling a little better about his position as class leader. As he set down his backpack to pull on his jacket, Dylan approached him.

"Bad news," Dylan said.

"What?"

"You just missed the bus. I was going to tell the driver you were talking with the teacher, but the bus pulled away before I could get there."

Christopher picked up his backpack and hoisted it over his shoulder. "It's okay. I can catch a ride home with my brother."

Dylan walked with Christopher to the high school, and then they parted ways by the front door. Christopher ducked inside just as the bell rang and plastered himself against the wall as students spilled out of their classrooms and into the hallway. He'd learned the hard way that he didn't want to be caught up in the middle of the tide.

As the crowd of students subsided he slowly inched his way toward Sam's locker. By the time he reached it, Sam was already there, shoving his books inside.

Arielle stood beside him, wearing a brown vest and a turquoise shirt that matched her earrings. Neither of them noticed Christopher standing behind them.

"Are you ready for the big ACT test tomorrow?" Arielle asked Sam.

He shrugged. "Ready as I'll ever be. I can't believe I have to take a four-hour test on a Saturday morning. Who came up with that lamebrain idea?"

"At least we can go shopping afterward."

"I guess so." Sam dropped a notepad on top if his books. "Does that mean you're still planning to ride to Harding with me?"

She nodded. "The test starts at eight and we absolutely can't be late, so let's leave by seven. And don't forget that you need to bring *two* number-two pencils and your driver's license with you to be allowed into the testing center."

"I know," Sam told her.

Arielle hugged her books against her chest. "I'm so nervous. I need to score at least a 20 to be accepted to the University of Nebraska."

"You'll get that easy," Sam assured her. "You're smart."

She smiled. "So are you. I just hope you don't beat my score." Then she glanced over her shoulder and saw Christopher. "Hey, how long have you been standing there?"

Christopher shrugged. "I don't know. I missed the bus."

"Again?" Sam closed the locker door and rolled his eyes.

"I'll see you later," Arielle said, giving them both a wave as she headed down the hallway. "Call me."

"I will." Sam picked up his backpack and headed toward the door. "So how was school?"

"Okay." Christopher took long strides to keep up with his big brother. "I got picked to be the class leader for the canned food drive."

"That should be fun."

"I guess."

When they reached Sam's car, Christopher got into the passenger side of the Datsun 240-Z and unspooled the seatbelt. "So where do you want to go to college, Sam?"

Sam shook his head. "I have no idea."

Just as Christopher opened his mouth to ask another question, Sam turned on the radio and blasted the volume so loud it hurt Christopher's ears.

Chapter Three

Charlotte stood at the kitchen counter slicing leftover roast beef when Christopher burst through the door with Sam lagging behind him.

"Hey, Grandma," Christopher greeted her. "Uncle Pete is outside yelling at the combine. I think it broke down again."

Charlotte set the knife down on the cutting board. "Oh, dear. Do you know what's wrong?"

Sam slipped his backpack off his shoulder. "Nope, but Uncle Pete was kicking the tire and calling it a piece of junk."

She sighed, understanding his frustration. Breakdowns always meant delays, which could result in a loss of yield and income. She just hoped whatever part the combine needed this time didn't have to be ordered.

Charlotte looked over at Sam, who was digging into the cookie jar. "If AA Tractor Supply doesn't have the part he needs, maybe you could pick it up in Harding after soccer practice."

"We don't have practice tonight," Sam told her. "The coach has a wedding or something."

Charlotte glanced at the slices of roast beef she'd planned to make into sandwiches. "If the combine isn't running, I guess I won't have to take supper out to the field tonight."

Bob walked through the door and confirmed the change of plans as he hung his cap on the hook. "We'll be eating here, Charlotte. We're done harvesting for today."

"What happened?" Charlotte asked him.

"The drive belt broke. Pete's on his way to Tractor Supply to pick one up."

"I hope they have one in stock," Charlotte said.

"We'll find out soon enough," Bob replied. "If they do, we'll put the belt on tonight after supper so she'll be ready to go again in the morning."

Charlotte picked up the knife again. "Well, it sounds like the repair won't be too costly this time."

"It could be a lot worse," Bob agreed. Then he motioned for his grandsons. "Time to do your chores. It'll be dark soon."

Bob and the boys headed outside while Charlotte finished preparing supper.

SINCE THEY WERE EATING in the kitchen tonight instead of the field, she warmed up the roast beef in the oven and roasted some onions and carrots to go along with it. She'd made a batch of coleslaw this morning and rounded off the meal with a jar of her home-canned dill pickles and a fruit salad.

By the time she finished setting the table, Emily and the

boys were cleaning up while Bob and Pete poured themselves cups of fresh-brewed coffee.

"Did you get the drive belt?" Charlotte turned to her son.

"I sure did," Pete said. "It was the last one Brad had in stock too."

The family sat down at the table while Charlotte retrieved the dinner rolls from the oven and placed them in a basket. She set it on the table and slid into her chair as Bob lowered his head to say grace.

"Heavenly Father," Bob intoned, his gnarly hands folded in front of him, "we thank thee for this bountiful food and for all the gifts you've given to us. May we use them to do thy will. Amen."

"Amen," Charlotte echoed, before picking up her napkin and laying it across her lap.

"Hey, save some of that roast beef for the rest of us," Sam told Pete as he watched his uncle layer his plate with thick slices of meat.

"Don't worry." Pete laughed. "I'll leave a scrap or two for you."

Charlotte took a warm roll from the basket, enjoying the easy banter at the dinner table. She split the roll with her fingers and then began to butter it.

"Besides." Pete continued to heap his plate full. "How hungry can you kids get just sitting around that school all day? I actually work for a living."

"School is a lot of work too." Emily scooped a large spoonful of carrots and onions onto her plate. "I had a geometry test today and a history test, but you can have all the roast beef you want." She wrinkled her nose at the platter of meat.

"I'm sure glad Dana's not as picky as you," Pete said. "I know she'll love whatever Mom cooks tomorrow night."

"Tomorrow night?" Charlotte echoed. "Is Dana joining us for supper?"

Pete looked at her in surprise. "You told me to invite her and her folks for an engagement dinner. It's all set. Her grandma will be coming too."

Panic gripped her. "Pete, I told you to ask them to join us *next* Saturday night. I need time to get the house and the yard ready for company."

"Oh, Mom," Pete said with a dismissive wave of his fork. "The place looks fine. Dana said her parents are so excited about the engagement dinner that they're driving from Grand Island to Bedford tonight to stay with her for the weekend."

Charlotte slumped back in her chair, her mind whirling. If the Simonses were already on their way to Bedford, then it was too late to postpone the engagement dinner. She'd just have to find a way to pull it all together.

"Okay, everybody," Charlotte announced. "Cancel all your plans for tomorrow. If we want to make a good impression, we have a lot of work to do."

"Sorry, Grandma," Sam said between bites of roast beef. "I have to go to Harding to take the ACT test tomorrow morning. I already paid the fee and everything."

Charlotte sighed. "You're right. You need that test to apply for college."

"And I promised Miss Middleton I would help her with

housework tomorrow afternoon," Emily said. "Should I call her and tell her I can't do it?"

"No," Charlotte replied, sending a beseeching look to her husband. "If you already made the commitment, you need to stick to it."

"I can help you, Grandma," Christopher said cheerfully. "Dylan and Wyatt can help too. They're coming over tomorrow, remember?"

Charlotte stifled a groan, having forgotten all about the Saturday play date the boys had set up. She knew all too well that Christopher and his two friends would probably end up making more work for her rather than less. An old nugget her grandpa used to say about hiring boys to work on the farm ran though her head: *A boy is a boy. Two boys is half a boy. Three boys is no boy at all.*

"Thank you, Christopher," she said, appreciating his offer of help all the same.

Pete wiped his mouth with his napkin. "I'd pitch in if I didn't have to harvest. It's supposed to rain next week, and I'm hoping to get the last of the corn picked on the Sawchuck Quarter while the ground is still dry."

Charlotte sighed as her gaze moved to her husband. "And I suppose you need to drive truck for him?"

"Yep," Bob replied. "Why don't you just plan this dinner for another day if it's going to be too much work?"

It wasn't the work that bothered Charlotte. She just wanted to make the occasion as special as possible. The thought of postponing the engagement dinner after Pete had already issued the invitation just didn't sit well with her.

"No, we'll go ahead and have the engagement dinner tomorrow night," Charlotte replied, squaring her shoulders. "I'll give Bill a call later this evening and ask them to join us."

Pete grinned. "Then it's all set."

She gave him a wry smile, wondering if her younger son had any idea what it took to throw a successful dinner party, especially on such short notice. She didn't even have a menu planned.

"I can dust and vacuum for you tonight, Grandma," Emily offered.

"Thank you," Charlotte said, touched by her granddaughter's thoughtfulness. "That would be very helpful."

Sam grinned. "I'll be happy to sample any food you make, Grandma."

Charlotte laughed. "I'm sure you would. Maybe I'll have you do the dishes while I start making pies."

He sighed. "I guess I could do the dishes, as long as I get to sample some pie when I'm done."

"What about me?" Christopher asked. "What do you want me to do, Grandma?"

Charlotte thought for a moment. "How about if you clean your room? The Simonses will probably want a tour of the house and farm, so it would be nice if all the rooms were clean."

Pete paled. "A tour? Does that mean they'll want to see my place too?"

"I expect so," Bob told him, spearing a pickle with his fork. "After all, that's where their daughter will be living after you're married."

"My apartment is a mess," Pete confessed. "I really haven't had time to clean it since we started harvesting."

Christopher's mouth gaped open as he turned toward his uncle. "You actually clean your apartment?"

The question made everyone laugh. They all knew Pete's apartment often looked like a disaster area. Charlotte had even been known to sneak in a time or two just to give it a quick going-over with her dust cloth.

Pete shrugged. "Like I said before, I'm a busy man. Cleaning doesn't pay the bills around here. I get to it when I can."

Charlotte knew that what his bachelor pad needed most was a woman's touch. The flowered wallpaper Bob's mother had hung forty years ago still decorated the living room, and in the kitchen, the linoleum was scarred and the cabinets outdated. She'd resisted making decorating suggestions to him, wanting to give Pete as much independence as possible while he lived on the farm. Once Dana moved in there, Charlotte was certain the apartment would look much nicer.

"I can try to straighten up the apartment for you tomorrow," Charlotte told him, mentally adding that task to her to-do list. "At least I can make it presentable for company."

"Thanks, Mom," Pete said. "I'll owe you one."

"Then it's settled." Charlotte placed her napkin on the table beside her, more focused on preparing the house for company than eating. "We'll have the engagement dinner here tomorrow night, and I'm going to make it as perfect as possible."

Chapter Four

The next afternoon, Charlotte grabbed the jar of sun tea that had been steeping on the front porch and carried it into the kitchen. She'd been moving in high gear since before dawn trying to prepare for the engagement party.

Unfortunately, Bill and his family would not be joining in the celebration. Bill had called this morning and said that Anna wasn't up to it. She'd been having a tougher time with this pregnancy than she'd had with the previous two and was really wiped out. Charlotte was disappointed, but she understood how tired a woman could be late in pregnancy, especially when she had other children to care for.

Charlotte poured the tea into a green glass pitcher and then added some ice cubes before placing the pitcher in the refrigerator. Without pausing, she walked over to the table and checked off "make sun tea" from the list she'd written last night to help keep her on schedule today.

She glanced over at the clock, noting that her guests were due to arrive in a little more than an hour. As she checked over the rest of her list, a knock sounded at the back door.

"Come on in," Charlotte called, preparing to check off another item on the list when Hannah walked inside the kitchen.

"Sorry it took me so long." Hannah carried a cardboard box in her arms and wore a smile on her face. "Frank wanted my help moving the grain truck to another field, and you know how these farmers are during harvest time. They just can't wait."

"I know," Charlotte said, clearing off the table. "But you're right on time. I was just getting ready to set the table."

Hannah placed the box on the kitchen counter and then pulled out a lace tablecloth that was folded into a neat square. "I just pressed this, so it shouldn't have too many wrinkles. Let's give it a good shake."

Charlotte walked over to grab one end of the lace tablecloth while Hannah held on to the other. They shook it out and then carried it over to the table.

"It's so beautiful," Charlotte said, her fingers smoothing over the feathery, hand-crocheted white lace. "Thank you for letting me borrow it."

"I'm happy to do it. We don't have too many fancy dinners at our place, so I'm glad someone can put it to good use."

Charlotte sighed. "This engagement dinner won't be too fancy, but I've prepared plenty of food. I made a couple of pies last night, and I've got two more baking in Pete's apartment because I ran out of room in my oven."

Hannah inhaled deeply. "Well, fancy or not, it sure smells good in here."

"Thanks," Charlotte said as she gently tugged one edge of the lace tablecloth to even it out. "I just want to make this engagement dinner special for Pete and Dana."

"Are you nervous?"

Charlotte walked over to the cupboard and took down a stack of her best plates. "A little, although I'm looking forward to getting reacquainted with Chuck and Bonnie."

"That will be nice." Hannah pulled two tapered ivory candles from her box. "How long have they been gone from Bedford?"

Charlotte thought for a moment. "Chuck took that insurance job in Grand Island right after Dana graduated from high school, so I guess it's been at least fifteen years."

"You'll have a lot of fun catching up," Hannah said. "Between that and talking about the wedding, your dinner party is sure to be a big success."

Charlotte smiled, grateful for Hannah's words of encouragement. *Thank you, Lord, for giving me such a wonderful friend.*

As Charlotte began setting her best plates around the table, Hannah picked up Charlotte's two silver candleholders, set them on the center of the table, and gently inserted a candle into each one.

"Those look great. You saved me by bringing those candles," Charlotte said.

Hannah smiled, "Glad to be of service," she said

Hannah helped Charlotte finish setting out the plates, glasses, and silverware. Then she stepped back and emitted a wistful sigh. "The table looks lovely, Charlotte."

"Wait until you see the finishing touch." Charlotte walked over to the refrigerator and pulled out a bouquet of fresh flowers.

"Where did you get those?" Hannah asked as Charlotte set the bouquet of red Gerbera daisies accented with wisps of white baby's breath in the center of the table.

"I had Emily pick them up at Filly's Flower Shop while she was in town. I know I shouldn't have spent the money, but I decided to splurge a little since this is such a special occasion."

"It was definitely worth it. The flowers make a perfect centerpiece."

Charlotte hoped Bob felt the same way, but it was too late to worry about that now. A loud clatter above them made both Charlotte and Hannah look up toward the ceiling.

"What have you got up there," Hannah asked over the noise, "a herd of wild horses?"

"Worse," Charlotte said with a wry smile. "Three eleven-year-old boys. They're supposed to be picking up Christopher's room."

Hannah grinned. "Sounds like they decided to tear it apart instead."

The clatter grew even louder as the three boys ran down the stairs and into the kitchen with Christopher leading the way.

"My room is clean now," he announced, skidding to such a sudden stop that Dylan and Wyatt both bumped into him. The three boys exploded in laughter.

"I'm glad to hear it," Charlotte said, although she questioned whether she and the boys shared the same definition of *clean*. Still, she didn't have time to check for herself, so she'd have to take Christopher's word for it.

"What else do you want us to do, Grandma?" Christopher asked.

"Why don't you crush the empty pop cans I found in Pete's apartment when I cleaned it this morning?" she suggested, hoping that if she kept the boys busy they'd stay out of trouble.

With any luck, Dylan's mother might already be on her way to the farm to pick up Wyatt and Dylan. "There are two sacks of cans right by his door."

"Wow," Dylan exclaimed, turning to Christopher. "Your uncle must really like pop."

"He does," Christopher affirmed. "There's so much root beer in his refrigerator that it takes up one whole shelf."

Wyatt wrinkled his brow in confusion. "So why do you crush pop cans?"

"We crush them to make them smaller," Christopher informed him. "Then we put them in a big trash barrel out in the shed. When the barrel is full, my Uncle Pete takes all the cans to a recycling place in Harding. He gets money for them and then lets me and Sam and Emily split it."

"Cool," Wyatt exclaimed as the boys headed for the door. "Let's have a contest to see who can crush the most pop cans the fastest."

"I bet I can crush two of them at the same time if I jump on them with both feet," Christopher shouted as the boys raced outside.

"Oh, my," Hannah said with a bemused smile. "Looks like you've had your hands full today."

"Actually, it was kind of nice that the boys were here to keep Christopher company since Emily and Sam were out most of the day."

As soon as she said his name, Sam walked through the back door.

"Hey, Grandma." Sam nodded toward Hannah. "Hi, Mrs. Carter." Then he turned toward Charlotte. "Is supper almost ready? I'm starving."

"We'll be eating soon," Charlotte told him. "How did the test go?"

He shrugged. "Okay, I guess."

"Was it hard?" Hannah asked him.

Sam opened the refrigerator and peered inside. "The science part was the worst. They have these long sections where you have to read about some weird experiment, and then you have to look at the data table and answer a bunch of questions about it."

"That doesn't sound like a fun way to spend a Saturday," Hannah said.

"Believe me, it's not," Sam replied as he closed the refrigerator and then headed over to the cookie jar and opened the lid.

Hannah smiled as she watched Sam pull out three chocolate chip cookies. "You're going to ruin your appetite, young man."

"I don't think that's possible," Charlotte said ruefully as she watched Sam devour a cookie in two bites. "His stomach seems to be a bottomless pit."

"Hey, I'm still growing," Sam said in his own defense.

"Well, when you finish the cookies, why don't you go upstairs and change clothes?" Charlotte told him. "I want everyone to look nice for dinner."

He frowned. "You mean I have to dress up?"

"Nothing too fancy," she assured him. "Just wear your church clothes. Emily's already up there getting ready."

"Okay, if you insist." Sam popped the last cookie into

his mouth and then headed toward the stairs. "But I bet Uncle Pete will be wearing jeans."

"That's a bet he might win," Charlotte told Hannah when Sam was out of earshot. "Although I tossed most of Pete's jeans into the washing machine when I went over this morning, so at least they'll be clean."

Charlotte heard the rumble of the combine and walked over to the window to look outside. "Looks like Bob and Pete are back from the field."

Hannah moved toward the door. "I'd better skedaddle since your company will be here soon."

"Thanks again for bringing over the tablecloth and candles. You're a lifesaver."

"Just give me all the juicy details about the engagement dinner the next time we talk. I can't wait to hear how it goes."

A few minutes after Hannah left, Bob walked inside. "Smells good in here. I'm starved."

"You'll have just enough time to clean up before Dana's family gets here," Charlotte told him. "Remember, wear a coat and tie. I want all of us to look nice tonight."

Bob grunted a reply as he headed toward the bedroom. He sounded no happier than Sam had about the dress code, but Charlotte knew he would comply.

She took one last look around the kitchen and then checked her list. The only items left to be marked off were the two pies baking in Pete's kitchen. They'd be done in a few minutes, giving Charlotte enough time to bring them back to the house to cool while she changed clothes for dinner.

As she headed outside, Charlotte didn't see or hear Christopher and his two friends. She knew that was probably a bad sign, but she didn't have time to investigate. She'd already given Christopher instructions that he was to change into his good clothes as soon as Dylan and Wyatt left.

She walked over to the tractor shed and climbed the stairs to Pete's apartment. The door was open and she could hear the shower running in the bathroom. The aroma of cherry-berry pies filled the air.

Charlotte moved into the small kitchen and opened the oven door. The flaky pie crusts were a perfect golden brown. Pulling on a pair of oven mitts, she carefully took each pie out of the oven and placed it on top of the stove.

As she pulled off the oven mitts, Pete emerged from the bathroom with a towel wrapped around his waist. "Hey, Mom, I thought I heard you out here. Do you have time to iron this shirt for me while I shave? I've got the ironing board already set up in the living room."

Charlotte took one look at the wrinkled blue dress shirt in his hand and knew she couldn't refuse. She took it from him and walked over to the ironing board. She plugged in the iron, wishing he'd told her about his wrinkled shirt before now.

At thirty-four, her son should be doing his own ironing, but she knew how busy Pete had been with the harvest and that he'd worked hard all day to finish in time for this dinner. Besides, before long he'd be getting married and wouldn't need his mother to do his last-minute ironing anymore.

She licked her index finger and tapped it against the surface of the iron, pleased to hear the tiny sizzle that indicated it was hot. Spreading the shirt over the ironing board, she quickly pressed it, steaming out the wrinkles in the fabric and snapping a stray thread from the collar.

"There you go," Charlotte said as Pete emerged from the bathroom once more, this time with his face freshly shaved.

"Thanks," he said, taking the shirt from her and pulling it on. "And thanks for cleaning up my apartment. It looks great."

Great wasn't exactly the word Charlotte would use to describe the place. She looked around, trying to see it through the eyes of Dana's mother. "You know, you might want to paint the living room this winter. That would really freshen it up."

Pete buttoned his shirt cuffs. "That's not a bad idea. I think Dana mentioned the same thing the last time she was over here."

Charlotte walked back into the kitchen and loaded the hot pies into the pie carrier Pete had made for her pie business last year. "Come over to the house as soon as you're ready."

"I'll be there in a few minutes," he promised.

Charlotte toted the pie carrier down the stairs and walked out of the tractor shed. The first thing she saw were three giant pyramids of pop cans standing in the middle of the driveway.

"What in the world?" she breathed, wondering how the boys had managed to erect the pyramids in the short time she'd been inside Pete's apartment.

"Christopher?" she called out, walking toward the house.

He suddenly appeared around the corner of the barn, his eyes wide and his cheeks flushed. "Grandma, something terrible has happened!"

Chapter Five

Charlotte's heart skipped a beat as she imagined the worst. As she ran up to Christopher, she berated herself for not keeping a closer eye on them.

"What is it?" she cried. "What happened?"

"The chickens are loose!"

She blinked, taking a moment to comprehend what he'd just said. Then she heard Toby barking and saw Dylan and Wyatt chasing a flock of unruly hens across the yard. Her shoulders relaxed.

"How did that happen?" Charlotte asked at last.

"I don't know," Christopher said with a shrug. "We went into the chicken house to see if there were any eggs because Wyatt's only seen eggs from the grocery store and he's never seen brown eggs before. Someone must have accidentally left the gate open."

Charlotte realized it didn't matter how it happened, she just needed to fix it. The sun was setting and loose chickens meant the coyotes would have a feast if they didn't get them locked safely back in the chicken coop. She knew Dana and her family were on their way, but she didn't have any choice other than to rush into the house and call for help.

"Bob!" Charlotte shouted as she ran into the kitchen and set the pie carrier on the counter. "Sam! Emily! I need you!"

"What is it?" Bob called as he emerged from the family room wearing a suit and tie.

Emily followed him in a pink dress with a pink-and-white-striped knit shrug.

Charlotte took a moment to catch her breath. "The chickens got out and we have to get them back in their pen as fast as possible. Where's Sam?"

"I'm right here," Sam announced as he walked into the kitchen wearing a dark blue polo shirt and khaki pants. "But I'm not really dressed right for a chicken hunt..."

"We don't have time for you to change," Charlotte interjected, heading for the door. "Dana and her parents will be here any minute."

The rest of the family followed Charlotte outside. Chaos reigned as Wyatt and Dylan chased chickens across the driveway. Toby had joined in the fun, barking and racing around the yard, making the chickens squawk and flap their wings.

"What a mess!" Emily exclaimed.

Christopher walked by with one of the hens tucked under his arm. "Hey, I got one!"

"You are going to be in so much trouble," Sam predicted as he planned his strategy. "I'll try to get the rooster. Maybe I can trap him behind the barn."

"Be careful," Emily warned. "He's a mean one."

Charlotte ran into the driveway, chasing after a young hen. She grabbed it off the ground by its feet and hung it upside down to keep it from pecking her. Then she snatched another hen that had stopped to peck at an empty root beer can.

Pete emerged from the tractor shed wearing his blue shirt and a striped tie. He shook his head when he saw all the commotion. "Who let the chickens out?"

"Christopher," Sam replied.

"It wasn't me," Christopher shouted in his own defense. He looked over at Dylan, who blushed, and then glanced back at Pete. "I'm not sure how it happened. The gate just didn't latch."

Pete scowled. "And why are there empty root beer cans all over the ground?"

"Stop talking and start helping," Charlotte told him. "Dana will be here any . . ."

Before she could even finish the sentence, Charlotte heard the sound of tires rolling over gravel. With a sinking heart, she looked up, hoping to see Brenda Lonetree's car on the road in front of the house. Instead, Dana's small red car pulled into the driveway.

"Great," Pete muttered.

Charlotte looked down at her clothes, a tiny spray of dirt splattered across the front of her old gray sweatshirt from the kicking hens in her hands. She'd be greeting Pete's future in-laws with dirty clothes, messy hair, and no makeup.

"They probably won't even recognize me," Charlotte muttered to herself.

Knowing she didn't have any choice, Charlotte handed the hens off to Emily and approached the car to greet her guests.

Chuck and Bonnie Simons emerged from the backseat of the car while Dana helped her grandmother Maxine, known as Maxie to everyone in Bedford, out of the front passenger seat.

"I know we're a little early," Dana said. "I was so excited for my folks to see the changes to Heather Creek Farm since the last time they were here . . ." Her voice trailed off as a squawking chicken darted under her car.

Wyatt chased after it, diving onto his stomach and wiggling underneath the vehicle. "Here chicky, chicky."

"I have to apologize," Charlotte said as Wyatt wiggled farther under the car until only his white tennis shoes were visible. "I'm afraid . . ."

"Here, chicky, chicky," Wyatt crooned.

Charlotte sighed. "I'm afraid the chickens got out, and we have to get them all back inside the coop before dark."

Maxie Simons began to chuckle. "Brings back old memories."

"It sure does," Chuck said, smiling down at his mother. He was a tall man with a lanky build and a deep cleft in the center of his chin.

Charlotte took one look at Bonnie and knew what Dana would look like in twenty years. Bonnie's dark hair was short and stylish, and a twinkle lit her blue eyes as she surveyed the scene.

"We can help," Dana offered, before making quick introductions. "Charlotte, you remember my mother, Bonnie, and my father, Chuck. And of course you already know my Grandma Maxie."

"Of course," Charlotte said as Wyatt disappeared completely under the car.

"Here chicky, chicky," he called.

Charlotte bent down to look at him. "Wyatt, why don't you come out of there? We'll get the chickens."

"I got him," Wyatt shouted. Then he yelped as the chicken began to squawk. "No, I don't."

The panicked hen flew out from underneath the front bumper of the car and Dana pounced on it, grabbing the chicken as it flapped wildly in her arms and sprinkling dirt across the front of her pink dress.

"Oh, Dana," Bonnie said, taking a step back. "Be careful."

"Here, I'll take it," Charlotte offered, plucking the chicken out of Dana's tenuous grasp. "I'm so sorry about your dress."

"It's okay," Dana said, giving her a weak smile. "A little dirt won't hurt me. I guess I'd better get used to it if I'm going to live on a farm."

"It probably won't hurt your dress either," Grandma Maxie told her granddaughter. "Just brush it off. It probably won't even leave a stain."

Charlotte noticed that most of the chickens had been caught and the boys were now picking up all the pop cans. She motioned for Emily to come and take the remaining hen from her.

"This is my granddaughter, Emily," Charlotte said, handing over the chicken. "She's a sophomore this year at Bedford High."

Emily grimaced as she held the chicken as far away from her as possible, trying not to soil her favorite dress. "Nice to meet you," she said.

"It's nice to meet you too, Emily," Bonnie said with a smile.

Charlotte motioned them toward the house. "Why don't we go inside? Dinner is almost ready."

As she escorted them toward the house she saw Brenda Lonetree pull into the driveway to pick up Wyatt and Dylan. Bob brought the boys to the car and talked to Brenda for a moment before the car pulled out again.

When they reached the door, Bonnie suddenly stopped. "Oh, I almost forgot. I brought you something."

She hurried back to the car and retrieved a bag from the backseat while they waited on the porch. Bob and Christopher soon joined them there.

"Nice to see you again, Bob," Chuck Simons said, reaching out to shake his hand. "How have you been?"

"Just fine," Bob said. "Nice to see all this commotion didn't scare you away."

Chuck smiled. "We don't scare easily. Although I did have a run-in with a rooster when I was ten years old and still have the scars to prove it. Remember, Mom?"

"I surely do." Maxie reached up to pat her salt-and-pepper hair, which was pulled back in a bun. A cheerful woman with a passion for cultivating roses, she often adorned the sanctuary of the Bedford Community Church with her prizewinning flowers.

Bob pointed toward the shed. "Our oldest grandson, Sam, is rounding up the rooster right now. I guess we'll see who wins that battle."

Bonnie returned to the porch holding a plastic grocery sack. "Here you go," she said, handing it to Charlotte.

Charlotte was touched by the gift, although the bag was so heavy she almost dropped it. "You didn't have to bring anything."

Then she looked inside and saw assorted cans of green beans, tuna, and pears. It was the most unusual hostess gift she'd ever received.

"Well, this is . . . very nice," Charlotte said, wondering if they expected her to serve any of it for dinner. "Thank you. We love green beans."

"Well, good," Bonnie said. "We weren't sure how much you needed, but you can never give too much to charity."

Bob scowled. "Charity?"

Christopher stepped forward. "I think those cans are for me." He looked up at Charlotte. "Miss Simons called while you were cleaning Pete's apartment and asked if she could bring anything."

Dana brought a hand to her mouth to hide a smile. "Oh my, I think there's been a misunderstanding. Christopher asked us to bring cans to donate to his class for the canned food drive."

Charlotte laughed along with the rest of them. "Well, that makes more sense." Then she turned to her grandson. "You never said anything about a canned food drive."

"I guess I forgot to tell you," Christopher shrugged. "The school is having a contest and the class with the most cans will win a field trip. I got chosen leader for my class, so I'm in charge of making sure we get enough cans to win."

Bonnie blushed as she looked at Charlotte. "You must have thought I was crazy." She reached into her purse and pulled out a small red box wrapped with a bow. "I did bring a hostess gift to thank you for having us here for dinner. I made it. I hope you like it."

Charlotte opened the box and pulled out a bracelet made of silver and abalone beads. "It's lovely. Thank you so much."

"You're welcome," Bonnie said. Then she turned to Christopher. "And I think it's so nice that a boy your age is helping people and taking a leadership role. I'm sure it will be a wonderful experience for you."

"I didn't really have a choice," Christopher admitted. "Miss Luka pulled my name out of a shoebox, so that means I'm class leader."

Chuck laughed. "Sometimes I wish we could choose our politicians that way. We might get more done that way."

Bob put a hand on Christopher's shoulder. "Even if a person doesn't want to do something, he should still give it his best."

"That's right," Grandma Maxie concurred. "I never wanted to clean chickens when I was a girl, but I did it anyway and always got a great reward at the end of the day."

Christopher squinted up at her. "You had to clean a chicken?"

"Well, I had to pluck all the feathers off the chickens when my mother was butchering them. It was a hard job and a messy one too."

"So what was your reward?" Emily asked as they entered the house.

Grandma Maxie grinned. "Fried chicken for supper."

Chapter Six

"Thanks for letting me clean up in here," Dana said as she stood in Emily's room.

"No problem." Emily sat on her bed watching Dana comb her hair. "I'm just glad you were able to get the dirt off your dress."

"Me too." Dana set the comb on the dresser. "I guess Grandma Maxie was right. It just scraped right off." She looked down at the bodice of her dress. "I can't see any stain, can you?"

"Not from here." Emily folded her legs underneath her. "Luckily that chicken didn't scratch you and make a hole in the fabric."

Dana sighed as she surveyed herself in the mirror. "I don't think I'll make a very good farm wife. I'm not used to chasing chickens around."

Emily laughed. "I wasn't used to it either until I moved here. In fact, I'm not sure I ever saw a real live chicken up close and personal before I came to Heather Creek Farm."

"Now the big question: are we eating one of those chickens for supper?"

"No." Emily shook her head. "I think Grandma made a pot roast."

Dana walked over and sat on the bed beside her. "I guess that's another thing I'll have to get used to as a farm wife—eating the animals grown on the farm. I'm used to seeing meat in the grocery store and not really thinking about where it comes from."

"That's why I'm glad I'm a vegetarian."

Dana smiled. "That's right. I forgot. Is it hard being a vegetarian when you live on a farm?"

Emily shrugged. "Not really harder than anywhere else. Grandma doesn't really bug me about it, other than making sure I'm getting enough to eat. I love eggs and peanut butter, so I get enough protein, and there's always something for me to eat."

"Well, you sure look healthy."

Emily nodded. "So, have you picked out a wedding dress yet?"

"Not yet. I've looked around some, but I want to find the perfect one. It's a once-in-a-lifetime decision, you know?"

Emily nodded, her eyes growing wide at the thought. "There are so many styles and colors too. Do you want white or ivory?"

"I don't know," Dana replied. "I think I'm going to have to try on some dresses before I decide." Then she looked up at her. "Maybe you can come with me when I go shopping."

Emily's mouth dropped open. "Are you serious?"

"Of course. You've got great taste in clothes. I'd really value your opinion."

"That would be awesome."

"Great," Dana exclaimed. "I've got a bunch of wedding magazines at home. We can look at those first and get some ideas. I don't want to be overwhelmed by all the choices when we walk into the bridal salons."

"Are you girls about ready?" Pete shouted up the stairs. "We're getting hungry down here."

"We'll be down in a minute," Dana shouted back. Then she rose to her feet. "I guess we should go downstairs, but I'd rather stay up here and talk about wedding dresses."

Emily laughed. "Me too. Have you picked your colors yet?"

Dana shook her head. "I'm leaning toward some shade of blue, but I could easily change my mind. Besides, I promised Pete I wouldn't make any final decisions until he's done with harvest and we have time to plan the wedding together."

"Are you sure about that?" Emily asked, pushing herself up off her bed. "Have you seen his apartment? He's not exactly a great decorator."

Dana chuckled. "Well, I'm sure I want him involved in the planning. As far as the apartment goes, I have some ideas for that as well, but I'd better wait until we're married to tell him all my plans."

"That's probably smart," Emily agreed as she moved toward the door. "I have to say it's going to be a little weird to have one of my teachers in the family."

"A little weird for me too, but I'm sure we can handle it." Dana headed for the stairs. "I suppose we'd better go down."

The phone rang, forestalling Emily's reply as she switched directions and moved toward the spare bedroom. "You go ahead. I'll answer it."

"Okay, I'll see you in a few minutes."

Emily walked into the bedroom and picked up the phone on the second ring. "Hello?"

"Hey, Em, it's Ashley."

"Hi, Ashley." Her voice was bubbly.

"Are you busy?"

"Well, kind of," Emily hedged. "Miss Simons and her family are here for an engagement dinner, and we're about to sit down to eat. I probably shouldn't talk too long."

"Okay, I won't keep you." She giggled. "I just wanted to tell you my news."

Emily sat down on the bed, intrigued by the tone of Ashley's voice. Something was definitely up. "What news?"

"Ryan asked me out on a date tonight."

Caught completely off guard by Ashley's announcement, Emily's mind went blank. "Ryan who?"

"Ryan Holt," Ashley said, as if the answer was obvious.

"Oh my gosh!" Emily's mouth fell open. "Are you serious?" Ryan Holt was a boy in their class. He was cute, if you liked the shaggy blond type. Smart too, although he preferred sprawling in his chair at the back of the classroom and making wisecracks instead of actually studying.

"Totally serious," Ashley said with a giggle. "I'm so nervous, Em. I think I'm going to be sick."

"You'll be fine," Emily assured her. "So what did he say? Give me all the details."

"I don't even remember," Ashley said. "I mean, I couldn't even believe Ryan was calling me, much less asking me for a date. You know how much I've always liked him."

Emily actually couldn't remember Ashley ever talking about him much before, except to say he told funny jokes in history class. "So he just called you out of the blue?"

"Weird, huh?" Ashley said. "I couldn't believe it either. I probably sounded like a complete idiot on the phone."

"I doubt that."

"He's picking me up at seven, and I have no idea what to wear." Ashley sounded a little breathless. "I'm sorting through my closet right now. I wish you were here to help me!"

Emily did too. She and Ashley shared everything together. "I'd love to come over, but I have to be at this engagement dinner for my uncle."

"I know. Just tell me if you think I should wear my black-and-red top with jeans or my silky blue blouse with jeans?"

Emily could hear the sound of hangers being pushed across a wooden closet rod. "They're both cute, but I like the blue one best. Where are you going?"

"To a movie in Harding. I thought my mom was going to say no when I first asked her." Emily looked closely at the blue blouse. "I would have died!"

"But obviously she's letting you go."

"It took a lot of convincing," Ashley said. "I have to stick to all of her rules, like getting home by eleven o'clock and carrying my cell phone with me so she can reach me at any time. It's a good thing she knows Ryan's parents or I think she definitely would have said no."

Ryan's father, Terrence Holt, was the president of the Great Plains State Bank in Bedford, and the family lived in one of the nicest houses in town. His mother, Stephanie, ran a small travel agency out of their home and wore the type of designer clothes that Emily dreamed of making someday.

"I have to go now and get ready," Ashley told her. "Wish me luck."

Emily gripped the phone tighter, feeling butterflies fluttering in her own stomach. "Good luck. Call me tomorrow and tell me everything."

"I will. Later, Em."

A dial tone sounded in Emily's ear, and she hung up the phone.

"Emily?" Charlotte called up the stairs. "We're all waiting for you."

"I'm coming, Grandma," Emily replied, heading for the stairs.

PETE TAPPED HIS COFFEE CUP with his spoon. "Can I have everyone's attention, please?"

Charlotte set down her fork. They were all seated at the table and just finishing up dessert. Bonnie Simons had been raving about Charlotte's cherry-berry pie while Bob and Chuck talked about the Husker football season.

Despite the rocky start to their evening, Charlotte thought the engagement dinner had been a great success. The two families fit together well, and Grandma Maxie had told stories that kept them all laughing throughout the meal.

Charlotte knew Pete was blessed to be marrying into such a fine, loving family, and she hoped Bonnie and Chuck felt the same way about Dana becoming a Stevenson.

"Dana and I have an announcement to make," Pete said, looking down at his fiancée.

Dana stood up beside him, hooking her arm through the crook of his elbow. Charlotte couldn't remember the last time Pete had looked so happy.

"We've set our wedding date," Pete said.

"Well, it's about time." Grandma Maxie slapped her hand on the tabletop. "An old woman like me can't wait forever. I'm getting up in years, you know. I don't even buy green bananas anymore."

Dana smiled lovingly at her grandmother. "Well, can you wait until March twenty-seventh? That's the day Pete and I are getting married."

"March twenty-seventh." Grandma Maxie nodded her approval. "I surely can. There's nothing I like more than a spring wedding."

"We'll just pray we don't get a spring blizzard," Pete said, circling his arm around Dana's waist.

"March weather is always unpredictable," Dana added, "but we wanted to be married before Pete gets too busy with the planting season."

"It sounds perfect to me," Bonnie told her daughter. "Although it doesn't give you two much time to plan a wedding."

"Well, we don't want anything too extravagant anyway," Dana replied. "Right, Pete?"

"That's right." Pete nodded.

Grandma Maxie breathed a wistful sigh. "I got married on Valentine's Day in my parents' parlor. It was so warm outside that we took our wedding picture in the gazebo my grandfather had built for his wedding. You'll never forget your wedding day, no matter how many years go by."

Charlotte nodded, remembering her own June wedding. That had been over forty years ago, but in some ways it seemed like yesterday.

She glanced at Emily, wondering if she looked forward to being a bride someday. Then again, most girls these days sought a career before a husband. Emily might do the same before she decided to settle down.

Dana and Pete would be awfully busy planning a wedding in four and a half months, but there was so much more to marriage than the wedding day. She prayed that

Pete and Dana's love would give them a strong foundation for a future together.

"Where are you going for your honeymoon?" Emily asked after the couple had resumed their seats. "Someplace fun like Hawaii or the Caribbean?"

Pete and Dana looked at each other.

"We haven't talked about it too much," Dana admitted. "I've collected some travel brochures and looked at some honeymoon resorts online."

"We can't go too far or be gone too long," Pete reminded her. "Calving season should be over by then, but I'll still need to tend to the livestock."

Emily wrinkled her nose. "You're getting married, and you're thinking about cows? That's not very romantic."

Grandma Maxie chuckled. "A farm wife learns to adjust to the seasons. And by seasons, I mean calving season in the winter, planting season in the spring, and harvest season in the fall."

"Don't forget irrigation season," Bob reminded her. "That takes up over half the summer. Then you've got to make some time for weaning calves and haying and making silage."

Chuck smiled at the expression on his daughter's face. "Don't worry, hon. I'm sure you'll have time to sneak in a honeymoon."

Charlotte looked across the table at her husband. "We went to Lincoln for our honeymoon."

Sam shook his head. "Wow, that sounds like a wild time."

"I suppose it's not like Hawaii," Charlotte admitted, "but it was fun at the time. We toured the capitol building and went fishing at Branched Oak Lake."

"I'd plan the wedding first, and then worry about the honeymoon," Bonnie advised them. "There are so many decisions to make. You need to get started right away, Dana."

"I know," Dana told her. "Pete will be done with harvest soon." She looked over at him. "Right?"

"Right," Pete confirmed. "Then I can give both the wedding and the honeymoon my full attention."

They continued to talk late into the evening until Grandma Maxie finally stood up and announced it was time to go.

"Some of us need our beauty sleep," Grandma Maxie said, leading the way to the door. "Thank you for dinner, Charlotte. I had a wonderful time."

"We loved having you," Charlotte replied. "You're welcome here anytime."

"You have to come to Grand Island and see us sometime," Bonnie said as they donned their coats. "We'd love to have you come to our place for dinner."

"We'll do that," Charlotte promised.

After they left, Charlotte turned to her family and breathed a sigh of relief. "Well, I think that went pretty well."

"See, Mom," Pete said with a wide smile. "I told you this dinner wouldn't be a problem. And you were so worried about it."

She looked up at her son, remembering the hours she'd spent cooking and cleaning, the runaway chickens, and the empty root beer cans scattered all over the driveway. The evening might not have been perfect, but she knew the memories would be.

"You're right, Pete" she admitted, knowing she'd do it all over again. "It was no problem at all."

Chapter Seven

On Monday morning, a loud clap of thunder rattled the windows as Charlotte finished packing Christopher's lunch. "Are you almost done with breakfast? The bus will be here soon."

"Almost," Christopher said, licking buttery toast crumbs off his fingers. "I still need to pack some cans to take to school for the food drive."

"Why don't you take the cans the Simonses gave you for today?" Charlotte suggested, setting his lunch bag next to him on the table. "Then I'll pack up another sack full of cans for you to take tomorrow. They're so heavy, one sack is probably all you'll be able to handle."

"Okay."

Charlotte reached out and smoothed a stray lock of his blond hair. "I'm proud of you for taking on this project, Christopher, even though I know you didn't really want to be the class leader. The Bible tells us to feed the poor, and you're living God's Word."

He looked up at her, his eyes wide. "I am?"

She grabbed her devotional book off the kitchen counter, and then slid into the chair next to him. Sam and Emily had already finished breakfast and gone upstairs to finish getting ready for school, and Bob was outside doing chores, leaving the two of them alone together in the kitchen.

"I was reading a passage from the book of Matthew this morning." She opened her devotional to the page she had read earlier. "Listen to what it says: 'Then the righteous will answer him, "Lord, when did we see you hungry and feed you, or thirsty and give you something to drink? When did we see you a stranger and invite you in, or needing clothes and clothe you? When did we see you sick or in prison and go to visit you?" The King will reply, "I tell you the truth, whatever you did for one of the least of these brothers of mine, you did for me."' That's Matthew 25, verses 37 through 40."

Christopher crinkled his brow. "What does that mean?"

"It means God wants us to take care of people who are hungry or thirsty or alone. Just like you're helping people who are hungry by collecting for the food pantry."

He looked up at her. "I guess that's pretty cool."

She laughed and kissed the top of his head. "It's very cool. Now, scoot. The bus will be here any minute."

Christopher grabbed his lunch sack off the table, and then went to the hall closet to retrieve his jacket. He zipped it up and pulled the hood over his head.

Charlotte looked out the front window and saw the school bus slowing down out on the road.

"Emily," she called up the stairs. "The bus is here."

Emily ran down the stairs, her jacket over one shoulder and her book-laden backpack dangling from her hand. "Bye, Grandma."

"Bye, Grandma," Christopher echoed, following his sister out the front door.

Charlotte stood in the open doorway and watched them walk across the lawn toward the road. Toby stood on the porch watching them as well, her tail wagging behind her. Thunder rumbled again in the cloudy sky above, but only a few drops of rain fell.

As the school bus pulled away from the farm, Charlotte closed the door, shivering a little as the cool, damp air permeated her red sweatshirt. Then she walked back into the kitchen and cleared the breakfast dishes off the table.

Sam walked into the room as she was wiping off the table with a damp dishcloth.

"Hey, Grandma," he said, holding up a large white envelope, "I forgot to give this to you."

"What is it?" she asked, taking it from him.

"An order form for graduation invitations." Sam slung his backpack over his shoulder, and then dug into the front pocket of his jeans for his car keys. "I think it's due tomorrow."

"Tomorrow?" she echoed. "That seems awfully early in the year to order invitations. You don't graduate for another six months."

"I know," Sam said with a shrug, "but Mr. Duncan said the deadline was firm."

Charlotte unfolded the order form, wondering how they were supposed to know how many invitations to order before they even started planning the party. She supposed this was no different than when Bill and Denise graduated from high school, but she honestly couldn't remember such an early deadline.

"I gotta go," Sam said, heading for the door. "See ya."

"Have a good day," she told him, her eyes still studying the form. The prices varied, depending on how many invitations you ordered, but they seemed awfully expensive to her.

Fat drops of rain began pelting the kitchen window pane, and Charlotte realized too late that Sam hadn't been wearing a coat when he left. She sighed, wondering why so many kids these days walked around without coats, even in inclement weather.

After she washed the dishes, Charlotte retrieved her baby-quilt blocks from her sewing bag and laid them out in neat rows on the kitchen table. Rainy days always seemed like the perfect time to do needlework, and she looked forward to working on the quilt for her precious new grandbaby.

As she studied the arrangement of the pieced blocks, the door opened and a gust of wind scattered half the fabric squares onto the floor.

"My word," Charlotte said as Bob and Pete walked into the kitchen. "When did the wind come up?"

"Just now," Pete said, taking off his farm cap and raking his hair back off his forehead. "And it brought rain and sleet with it."

Charlotte bent down to pick up the quilt blocks, grateful she'd mopped the floor last night after supper.

Bob walked over to the coffeepot. "Looks like I'll be working inside the house today. I want to go through all of the grain elevator receipts so I can figure out what the corn is yielding."

"I'm going to Harding," Pete told them. "Do you need anything there, Mom?"

Charlotte thought about it for a moment, and then shook her head. "I can't think of anything at the moment. I'm volunteering at Bedford Gardens today, so I can stop by Herko's if I need any groceries."

"Okay." Pete opened the cupboard and retrieved a travel mug from the top shelf. "I'll just fill up my coffee cup and head out."

She watched him pour coffee into the mug. "What are you going to do in Harding?"

"I thought I'd pick up some paint for my apartment. If the forecast holds true I won't be back in the field for a few days. That should give me enough time to paint the living room."

Charlotte nodded her approval. "That sounds like a good idea."

Bob snorted. "He's taking a risk, if you ask me. Dana probably won't like the color he picks out, and he'll have to paint it all over again after they're married."

"She'll like it," Pete said confidently. "We have the same taste."

Charlotte hoped he was right, but she was certain any color would be an improvement. "Will you be back in time for supper?"

"I should be," he replied. "If not, can you save a plate for me?"

"Sure thing," Charlotte said, waving to him as he walked out the door. Then she turned her attention back to her quilt project.

Bob scooted his chair back to make room for her to move around the table. "Looks like you're almost done."

She smiled. "I'm done sewing the pieces into blocks, but

now I need to add the appliqués and sew the blocks together, so I still have a long way to go."

"Hard to believe that baby will be here in another month."

"I know. I can hardly wait." She moved a couple of blocks around. "When I called Bill last Friday, he mentioned that he'll be stopping by sometime soon to pick up that baby stuff they have stored up in our attic."

"Their crib's up there, isn't it?"

"Yes, and their high chair and bassinet."

"Good thing they kept 'em." Bob took a sip of his coffee. "Kids cost enough money without having to buy all that baby stuff again."

His comment reminded her of the invitation order form Sam had given her earlier. She retrieved it from the counter and handed it to Bob.

"I don't know what to do," she said, as he looked over the form. "Those invitations are so expensive. They cost over two dollars apiece, and that's if you don't order anything extra, like the name plates or the embossed thank you cards."

Bob whistled low. "So how many do you figure we'll need?"

Charlotte took a moment to consider who they'd want to invite to Sam's graduation. "Bill and Anna, of course, and Hannah and Frank. I'd like to invite Melody too, and Pastor Evans and his family. There are several people in the congregation we'll want to invite, and most of our neighbors."

"In other words, it's going to add up."

She swallowed a sigh. *Why does everything have to cost so*

much? They'd already paid an arm and a leg for Sam's senior pictures. He still had to buy a graduation gown and cap, in addition to paying for college application fees and things like the ACT test.

"I'd say we'd want at least twenty-five invitations," Charlotte speculated, "maybe thirty. Better to have a few too many than to run out."

Bob sighed. "I guess you can go ahead and write the check for it."

Charlotte laid a hand on his forearm as another idea occurred to her. "Or we could make our own invitations. Julia Benson did that for her oldest last year, and they were so nice. She could probably tell me just how to do it."

"Are you sure you want to go to all that work?"

"It might be fun," Charlotte replied. "I'm sure Hannah will help me. I could probably recruit Dana too, since she'll be part of the family."

"That's right," Bob mused. "I guess she'll be living on the farm by the time Sam graduates from high school, won't she?"

Charlotte was looking forward to the opportunity to visit back and forth with her new daughter-in-law, although she intended to give the newlyweds plenty of privacy. She could remember her own days as a new bride on Heather Creek Farm and how Ma Mildred had made her a little nervous, although she'd loved her dearly.

Bob waved the order form toward Charlotte. "So what do you want me to do with this?"

"I'll take it," she said, holding out her hand. "I've got a box for all the letters and college brochures that have been mailed to Sam these past few months. I'll just stick it in there."

Bob handed it to her, and then turned toward the hallway. "I'll be at my desk if you need me."

Charlotte returned to her quilt blocks, neatly stacking them in a precise order so they were ready for the appliqués she'd cut out, following Rosemary's freezer-paper technique. With any luck, she'd be ready to sew the appliquéd blocks together to form the quilt top before it was time to leave for the Bedford Gardens Convalescent Center.

As she carried the blocks to her sewing machine, Charlotte wondered if Bill and Anna had picked out any names for the new baby.

"Thank you, Lord," she prayed out loud, "for bringing another little miracle into our family. Bless Anna and the baby and Bill and Jennifer and Madison. Please watch over them all, Lord, during this special time."

LATER THAT MORNING, Charlotte arrived at Bedford Gardens, brushing the raindrops off her jacket.

"Looks like it's a wet one out there," Anita Wilson said from her wheelchair. She sat by the front window, watching the rain fall.

"It certainly is," Charlotte agreed. "But it's better than snow."

"I hope I can still make it to church on Sunday mornings once winter arrives," Anita said wistfully. "I don't want to take a chance on breaking my ankle again. But it is awfully nice of Pastor Evans to arrange for the church van to pick up the parishioners living here. I always look forward to going to the worship service."

At eighty-seven, Anita was a faithful member of the Bedford Community Church and had been recuperating at Bedford Gardens since a fall last month.

"Any idea on when you'll be moving back home?" Charlotte asked her.

Anita sighed. "I hope just a few more weeks. I was really looking forward to spending Thanksgiving at home, but the doctor said my ankle won't be healed well enough then. The cook here is a sweet soul, but the menu gets a little bland for my tastes." She leaned forward. "I'll just assume this is where the Lord wants me to be for Thanksgiving and make the best of it. Maybe I can make someone else's holiday a little brighter."

Charlotte reached out to gently clasp her frail hand. Anita always gave so much of herself to the church and to the community that Charlotte wanted to give something back. "How about if I bring some Thanksgiving pies to brighten up the menu?"

Anita's eyes widened in delight. "Now that sounds like just what the doctor ordered. My mouth is already watering."

"Do you have any special requests?"

"Well, I do love your apple-caramel pie, but I don't want you to go to any trouble."

"No trouble at all. I'll have an apple-caramel pie fresh from the oven just for you on Thanksgiving Day. I'll bring some pies for the other residents too."

Anita squeezed her hand. "You're a good girl, Charlotte Coleman, just like your mother. I sure do miss Opal."

Charlotte smiled. It had been a long time since anyone

had used her maiden name. Precious memories of her mother flooded back. Although she'd lost her parents years ago, people like Anita were a special link to her family. "I miss her too."

Anita rolled her wheelchair away from the window. "Enough of this rain and foolishness. I have a birthday letter to write to my great-granddaughter. She's going to be six."

"Have fun," Charlotte said as Anita wheeled her way back to her room. Then Charlotte turned in the other direction and headed for the Alzheimer's ward to see if Greta Harbinger was there visiting her husband, Bud.

Bedford Gardens was composed of two wings with a central foyer and check-in desk in the middle. The Alzheimer's ward was a locked unit at the end of one hallway, and Charlotte had to press a special combination of numbers into the keypad for the door to open.

As she walked onto the ward, one of the residents waved to her from his wheelchair.

"Hello, Dalton," Charlotte greeted him. "How are you today?"

"I'm fine," Dalton said. "Just fine."

Dalton Bertrand had been the town's barber years ago and had given Charlotte a lollipop whenever she'd gone to his shop to watch her father get a haircut.

A friendly man, Dalton always waved to her when she came to volunteer at the convalescent home, although he could no longer remember her name.

Time might be moving fast for Charlotte and her family, but for the residents on the Alzheimer's ward, time had little meaning. Many of them could no longer grasp events from the past or the present, but they'd definitely taught Charlotte the importance of savoring each and every day.

Linda Lawrence, a nurse who worked the day shift on the ward, smiled as Charlotte approached the small nurses' station. "Hello, there."

"Hi." She slipped off her damp jacket, and then held it up with her bag. "Do you mind if I store these in the cupboard?"

"Not at all." Linda moved closer to the desk so Charlotte could squeeze behind her.

Charlotte opened the storage cupboard that lined the wall, and nestled her jacket and bag among the books and magazines inside. A colorful magazine cover caught her eye and she pulled it off the top of the stack.

"Oh, is this the new issue of *Memory Lane* magazine?" Charlotte asked her.

"It sure is," Linda replied. "We just got it in yesterday."

Memory Lane was filled with stories from decades past and brought so much joy to the residents. Even if they didn't remember parts of their own lives, the stories elicited a comforting familiarity that many seemed to enjoy.

"Is Greta Harbinger visiting today?" Charlotte asked, pulling it off the stack.

"You know, I think she actually took a day off. Must have had some errands to run," Linda told Charlotte.

Greta was a faithful caretaker of her husband, Bud, and Charlotte had grown quite fond of the two of them. She'd miss seeing Greta today.

"In that case, I think I'll start with a reading group this morning." Charlotte tucked the magazine under her arm and headed for the sunroom on the other side of the hallway. Several residents awaited her, some in wheelchairs and others using canes or walkers.

"Good morning, everyone," she said as she walked into the sunroom.

"Good morning, Charlotte," Bertha Webber said. She'd been placed in the home six weeks ago by her family, who had felt it was no longer safe to let her live at home. A former schoolteacher and lifelong resident of Bedford, seventy-three-year-old Bertha was in the beginning stages of Alzheimer's and still recognized most of her friends and family.

The sunroom was small, and the gentle patter of rain on the oversized window panes made it feel especially cozy today. Secured patio doors led to a fenced outdoor courtyard that the residents enjoyed in the warmer months.

Charlotte settled into a white wicker chair next to Bertha as other residents drifted into the room. "We've got some new stories to read," she announced as she opened the magazine. "The first one is called 'Penny Candy.'"

As soon as everyone was comfortably settled, she cleared her throat and began to read out loud: "Saving pennies used to really mean something back when I was a child in the 1950s. A penny could buy a sweet piece of taffy. A nickel could buy a candy bar, and a dime could buy a bottle of soda, with money back when you returned the empty bottle."

Bertha chuckled beside her. "I used to drink a bottle of my uncle's homemade ginger ale every Saturday night. My, but it tasted good."

Charlotte heard some of the other residents murmur in

agreement. This was the best part of story time for Charlotte, when a subject or article would spark a long-lost memory for one of the residents.

As she continued reading the story, she realized how even small things in life, like penny candy, could bring joy even years later. Memories might come and go, but God's love and mercy endured forever.

Chapter Eight

Emily walked into the school cafeteria at noon, scanning the room. Where was Ashley? She didn't have any classes with her in the morning, and her telephone had been busy when Emily tried to call her at home on Sunday.

The odor of meatloaf permeated the cafeteria, and she tried not to grimace as she approached the cash register line to pay for her carton of milk.

"Hey, Emily."

She turned around to see Hunter Norris standing behind her. He held a cafeteria tray, waiting to pay for his meal. The creamed peas and sliced peaches on his tray didn't look too horrible, but the sight of that thick slice of grayish-brown meatloaf swimming in a pool of grease turned her stomach.

"Hey, Hunter," she said, averting her gaze from his tray.

"I didn't think the lunch bell would ever ring," Hunter exclaimed. "I've been starving all morning."

"So how's Rambo?" Emily asked, eager to change the subject. She knew Hunter always liked to talk about his sorrel quarter horse.

"He's great." Hunter grinned. "I've been trying to ride him every day before the weather gets too cold. You should come over sometime. Maybe we could ride together."

Hunter and his family had moved to the old Schnurnberger place near Heather Creek Farm. It wasn't the first time he'd invited her to visit his farm, and she could tell he had a bit of a crush on her.

"Maybe," she said noncommittally, her gaze scanning the room. Ashley wasn't at their usual table, and Emily wondered for a moment if she'd stayed home sick from school.

"How about tomorrow after—" Hunter began.

"There she is!" Emily cut him off without even realizing it. She had finally spotted Ashley sitting at a table in the far corner of the cafeteria.

"Who?" Hunter asked, following her gaze.

"Ashley. I haven't talked to her since Saturday. It seems like forever."

Emily finally reached the cash register and dropped the coins for the milk carton in the lunch lady's outstretched hand. "See you later, Hunter."

"Okay," he said dully. "Bye."

Emily made a beeline for Ashley, wondering why she'd chosen to sit so far away from their usual table. As she got closer, she saw the reason why.

Ryan Holt.

Ashley was seated beside him. There were other kids seated there too, including Nicole Evans and Lily Cunningham. Emily slowed her step, uncertain if she wanted to join them. She and Nicole had never gotten along well and she'd already lost much of her appetite, thanks to the greasy meatloaf that Nicole's mom had probably cooked.

She turned around and had started walking away when Ashley called out her name.

"Emily! We're over here."

She hesitated, and then turned around again and plastered a smile on her face. "Hey," she said, surveying the crowded table. "Looks like you don't have room for me."

"Sure we do," Ashley countered, squeezing closer to Ryan and urging the student beside her to move down a spot.

Squaring her shoulders, Emily walked over to the table, aware of Nicole's critical gaze on her the whole time. The two of them had tangled more than once, and Emily usually tried to keep a good distance from her just to avoid any more conflicts. Emily knew Ashley didn't like either Nicole or Lily, so she was surprised to find her at the same table with them.

"Make room for the California girl," Ryan said, drawing laughter from the other kids. "Come on, Emily, sit down. We don't bite."

"Speak for yourself," Nicole said wryly.

Emily squeezed in beside Ashley and opened her sack lunch. She pulled out a peanut butter sandwich, a banana, and a small container of baby carrots.

"Look at little Miss Vegetarian," Nicole snickered. "You know, I've heard that awful things can happen to people who don't eat meat. Their skin gets all scaly like a lizard, and their hair starts falling out."

Emily opened her mouth to snap back a retort, but Ashley jumped in before she could speak.

"Oh, Emily's very healthy. Peanut butter has lots of protein in it, so I'm sure her hair and skin will be just fine."

Emily stared at her friend, wondering why she'd let Nicole off the hook so easily after such a nasty remark. No doubt Ashley was trying to keep the peace for Ryan and his friends.

It worked. Soon they were talking about the latest movies and how Harding needed to add more theaters if they didn't want kids to bypass them and go to the giant Cineplex in Grand Island.

Still stung by Nicole's insult, Emily sat in silence, taking small bites of her sandwich. The wheat bread tasted like sawdust in her mouth, and she had to take a large gulp of her milk just to swallow it without choking.

Nicole kept grinning at her from across the table, and Emily barely resisted the urge to reach over and slap her across the face. Grandma always told her she should turn the other cheek, but sometimes it was just *so* hard.

She munched on her carrots, listening to Ashley laugh at Ryan's jokes and wondering how she could feel so lonely at the most crowded table in the cafeteria.

LATER THAT EVENING, Charlotte sat in the family room with Bob dozing in his recliner. Sam had gotten home late from soccer and had just sat down at the computer, his hair still damp from his shower. Emily had gone up to her bedroom shortly after supper, and Pete still hadn't returned from Harding.

Charlotte glanced over to check Christopher's progress on his jigsaw puzzle, and then turned her attention back to the baby quilt on her lap. She'd finished appliquéing little ducks, boats, and hearts to several of the blocks and sewed the blocks together. Then she'd basted together the quilt top, batting, and backing. Now she was ready to start the actual quilting.

Suddenly a loud shout erupted from Sam. "Woo-hoo!"

Charlotte almost dropped her needle, and Bob bolted upright in his recliner, the newspaper sliding onto the floor.

The sound of footsteps clattered down the stairs, and Emily burst into the room, her eyes wide with apprehension. "Did something happen?"

"That's what I want to know." Bob scowled at Sam. "What are you caterwauling about?"

Sam grinned at him. "You're not going to believe it. I just got an e-mail from the soccer coach at Nebraska Wesleyan University in Lincoln."

Charlotte set aside the baby quilt and rose to her feet. "What does it say?"

Sam turned back to the computer and read the e-mail out loud: "Dear Sam, I received a video highlight tape from your soccer coach in Harding along with a recommendation that I consider you for our team. I was very impressed with your passing and shooting skills and your footwork. I'd like to invite you to Nebraska Wesleyan to tour the facilities and talk about finding a spot for you on our soccer team. Let me know if you're interested and we can set up an appointment. Coach Tucker."

"That's wonderful!" Charlotte exclaimed, knowing how much Sam wanted to play soccer in college.

"I can't believe it," Sam said. "I didn't think my coach even liked me, and here he's sending out highlight tapes."

"Nebraska Wesleyan's a private college, isn't it?" Bob asked.

"I believe so," Charlotte said. She knew private colleges were usually more expensive than public ones. "I'm sure they offer a lot of scholarships," she added quickly.

"Maybe I can get a full ride," Sam said, his face shining with excitement.

"Better see if you like the college first," Bob advised.

Sam nodded. "You're right. I know Jake and his parents are planning to go to the University of Nebraska-Lincoln for Red Letter Day next week. He invited me to go with them, but I wasn't really interested at the time."

Charlotte looked at her grandson. "Why in the world would you want to pass up that opportunity?"

Sam shrugged. "I don't know. It just didn't seem that important. But maybe now I can ride along and visit both colleges. I'm sure Jake won't mind touring Nebraska Wesleyan too."

Charlotte was happy to finally see her grandson excited about college. He'd been so ambivalent about where to go and what his major would be. She knew he couldn't major in soccer, but at least he was finally showing some enthusiasm.

"You're so lucky," Emily said wistfully. "I wish I could go off to college."

"Plenty of time for that," Bob told her. "You need to finish high school first."

"I'm going to give Jake a call right now," Sam said, rising from his chair. "If it's okay with him and his parents, then I can e-mail Coach Tucker back tonight and tell him when I'm coming."

Charlotte watched him bound out of the room, and then picked up her quilt project again. "Why don't you sit down by me, Emily," she said, patting the sofa beside her. "You can learn how to do quilting."

Ever since Emily had come home from school she'd seemed a little down in the dumps. Charlotte had asked her if anything was wrong, but Emily claimed she was fine. Then she'd gone outside to do her chores.

"Okay," Emily said, taking a seat next to her. She ran her fingers gently over the quilt top. "This is really pretty. I bet Uncle Bill and Aunt Anna will really like it."

"I hope so." Charlotte carefully transferred the project to Emily, and then pointed out where she'd made the last stitch.

"I hope I don't mess it up."

"You won't," Charlotte assured Emily. "Besides, we can always take the stitches out again and start over." She leaned closer to her to watch. "Now, push the needle through all three layers," she instructed. "Then come up through the top again. You need to make the stitches as small as you can. Just follow the blue quilting line I've marked there."

Emily nibbled her lower lip as she followed Charlotte's directions. "Like that?"

"Yes, that's very good."

Bob picked up the remote control and turned on the television. He flipped through the channels until he reached a popular game show.

"Oooh, I like this one," Christopher said, turning from his puzzle to watch the announcer tell contestants to, "Come on down!"

Several minutes later, Sam returned to the family room. "Well, it's all set. I'm going with Jake's family to Lincoln on Monday. We're leaving pretty early in the morning and probably won't be back until late that night."

"We'll have to write you a note for school so you can be excused on Monday," Charlotte told him. "Will you need to take anything with you to Lincoln, like your transcript or any teacher recommendations?"

"I don't think so," Sam replied as he walked over to the computer. "I have to sign up online for Red Letter Day at the University of Nebraska-Lincoln though, and I'm going to e-mail Coach Tucker and see if we can make an appointment for sometime on Monday afternoon."

Charlotte's attention moved back and forth from Sam typing at the computer, to Emily making tiny stitches in the quilt, to Christopher shouting out answers to the game show questions.

Bob was dozing once again in his chair, and Charlotte could hear the steady patter of rain on the roof. It had been raining most of the day, and she knew it would take a long time for the fields to dry out. Fortunately, Pete didn't have too much harvesting left to do.

She glanced at her watch, surprised to find that it was almost eight o'clock. *What's keeping Pete?*

Charlotte tried not to worry, knowing it was likely he had dropped by Dana's house on his way home from Harding or stopped in to watch *Monday Night Football* with Brad Weber. He'd have some free time for a few days until he could get back on the combine.

"There," Sam said, closing the open browser windows

on the computer. "The e-mail is sent, and I'm all signed up for Red Letter Day."

"You should let your Harding coach know about your invitation to visit Nebraska Wesleyan. I'm sure he'll be pleased."

Sam nodded. "Good idea. I still can't believe Coach Mendenhall sent a highlight tape of me anywhere. I told him I wanted to play college soccer, but we really didn't talk about it that much."

Before Charlotte could reply, Pete arrived at the house, barreling through the front door with a loud shout.

The noise startled Bob awake. "Now what's going on?"

Pete walked into the family room, a big grin spread across his face. "Wait until you see what I got."

Chapter Nine

They all followed Pete into the kitchen to see what he was so excited about. As soon as she walked into the room, Charlotte saw several sacks and boxes stacked by the door, droplets of rain still sticking to the surface of the packages.

"What is all this?" Bob asked, moving closer to inspect the boxes.

"My renovation project," Pete announced.

Charlotte walked over and peered into one of the sacks. "You got wallpaper?"

"Yep." Pete walked over and pulled out a tube of wallpaper. "It's a wallpaper border. The saleswoman at the home store in Harding recommended it. She said it was a perfect match for the lavender paint I bought for the bathroom."

Emily grimaced. "*Lavender*? You're going to paint the bathroom lavender?"

"The saleswoman suggested it and showed me a color swatch. It's right here," Pete said, pulling a sample out of a box of paint cans. "It's going to look great."

"I thought you were just going to paint the living room," Charlotte said.

"I was, but the more it kept raining, the more time I figured I'd have to fix up the place, so I decided to go whole hog."

Emily walked over to Pete and compared the paint swatch to the wallpaper. "You know, this might look pretty good after all."

"Of course it will." Pete stuck the wallpaper border back in the box.

"Are you sure you want to paint the entire apartment?" Charlotte asked him. "You'll have to tape first and move furniture around and pretty much disrupt your life until it's all done."

"Yeah, but why not get the mess over with all at once? This way I won't have to paint again for years."

Charlotte had to admit to herself that he had a point. She couldn't remember the last time that apartment had been painted. Probably not since well before Pete had moved in.

Bob folded his arms across his chest. "What else did this saleswoman talk you into?"

Pete grinned. "Well, she talked me into some ceramic floor tile for the kitchen, a light fixture for the bedroom, and some new handles for the kitchen and bathroom cupboards and drawers."

Bob groaned. "Sounds like you bought out the store."

"Almost," Pete admitted. "When she started describing the importance of feng shui, I knew I was in over my head and decided to hightail it back to Bedford."

"Good decision," Bob said dryly. "Too bad you didn't leave sooner. It sounds like it was a pretty expensive trip."

"Well, I got some good discounts on just about everything," Pete countered, "and it's been awhile since I did anything to spruce up the place. Besides, I've been trying to figure out what to get Dana for Christmas, and it finally hit me that this was the perfect present, considering she'll be living there in a few months."

Emily clasped her hands together. "Oh, I think that is *so* romantic. I can make some new curtains for you, Uncle Pete, and some couch pillows to coordinate with the new paint colors."

"Now that's the kind of offer I like to hear," Pete exclaimed. "Who else wants to help with Dana's Christmas present? I could use a painting crew and somebody who's good with wallpaper."

"I'd help you, Uncle Pete," Christopher said, "but I'm already the class leader for the canned food drive, so I'd better just concentrate on that."

Charlotte held back a smile at his solemn expression. Ever since their talk this morning about living God's Word, Christopher seemed to be taking his leadership role more seriously. He'd told her that only half the class had brought cans of food today and that he was hoping for a much better turn out tomorrow.

"I guess I can help you out on the weekends," Sam said, "but I have too much homework to be of much use the rest of the week. Now that I'm getting ready to apply to some colleges, I should probably try to get a few of my grades up."

Charlotte pressed her lips together to keep from telling Sam that he should have been trying to improve his grades much earlier if he wanted to make a good impression on a college admissions officer. Instead, she'd have to be satisfied with the fact that he was finally planning to apply somewhere.

"I guess that leaves me," Bob told his son. "Although I'm not sure how you think you're going to finish harvest and take care of the livestock and paint and tile and wallpaper your apartment all before Christmas. Looks like a lot of work to me."

Pete bristled at his tone. "I'll get it done, even if I have to work day and night."

"I'm sure Dana will be thrilled," Charlotte said, trying to break the tension.

Pete's shoulders relaxed. "I hope so. It's a secret though, so nobody can say a word to her about it."

"Good idea," Bob told him. "That way if you don't get it all finished by Christmas, Dana won't be disappointed."

Pete shook his head. "Have some faith in me, Dad. I can handle it."

Charlotte stepped over to the refrigerator and pulled out the dinner plate she'd been saving for Pete. "Let me warm this up for you. You're probably hungry."

"Actually, I grabbed a bite before I left Harding," Pete told her. "I'll have it for lunch tomorrow. Right now, I want to haul all this stuff over to my place and get started."

"I'll help you carry it over," Sam offered.

"Great." Pete rubbed his hands together. "While you're there, you can help me move some of the furniture away from the walls too."

Sam nodded. "Okay, just let me grab my coat first."

Charlotte shook her head, bemused by his sudden concern about the weather.

After Pete and Sam left, Bob returned to the family room while Charlotte made hot cocoa for Emily and Christopher.

"This should help you sleep tonight," Charlotte told

them as she poured cold milk into a saucepan, then set it on the burner to heat. "There's nothing like a cup of hot cocoa on a cold, rainy night."

The kids waited at the table while she mixed the sugar and unsweetened cocoa together, and then she added the warm milk before pouring the mixture into two mugs. There was enough left over for Sam when he came back from Pete's apartment.

"Here you go." Charlotte set a mug in front of each of them.

"Thanks, Grandma," they said at the same time.

"You're welcome." Charlotte returned to the counter where she wiped up a couple of drops of spilled milk. The cocoa smelled so good she was thinking about making some for herself when Christopher spoke behind her.

"Grandma, remember I need to take more cans of food tomorrow."

"That's right. Thank you for reminding me."

She opened the cupboards above her and surveyed the selection of canned goods. Since this was Christopher's project, she should probably let him pick out the cans.

"What do you want to take?" she asked him.

"Beets," he said immediately. "All three cans . . . and both cans of sauerkraut . . . and the peas . . . and cans of stewed prunes if we have any."

Emily burst out laughing. "You're just picking all foods you don't like!"

"So?" Christopher retorted. "I don't like stewed prunes, but someone would if they were hungry enough and it's important to feed the hungry. It says so right in the Bible, right Grandma?"

"Yes, it does," she said slowly, knowing that Emily was right about his choices and trying to think of a way to explain to Christopher that he shouldn't let his own needs and wants come first when he was giving to others.

"Grandpa likes the prunes," Emily retorted, her hands cradling her mug of cocoa. "You're going to make him go hungry if you take them all away."

"I don't think we have to worry about that," Charlotte said wryly. Although Charlotte wasn't a big fan of canned sauerkraut or stewed prunes, they were two of Bob's favorites.

"You can take one of each can," Charlotte told him, "but let's add a little more variety to our donation. That way people will have more foods to choose from and everyone can find a favorite and avoid foods they don't like. Just because they need some help getting by doesn't mean we only give them things that we don't want."

"Okay," Christopher said, draining the last of his cocoa. "But I bet a lot of people at the food pantry like beets."

Charlotte sighed and began loading food into the sack, adding cans of corn and sliced peaches and chicken noodle soup.

Christopher walked over to set his empty mug by the sink. "That cocoa was really good, Grandma."

"I'm glad you liked it. Now it's time for you to get ready for bed, young man."

"I don't think the cocoa's made me tired enough yet."

She smiled at his stall tactic. "Well, tired or not, you have school tomorrow so you need to get to bed. I'll be upstairs in a little bit to tuck you in."

"Okay," he said with a long sigh, surrendering to the inevitable.

Emily soon followed him upstairs, and Charlotte washed out their mugs before setting them in the dish drainer to dry.

She looked at the rain-streaked window over the sink, the dark night lit by occasional flashes of lightning. Thunderstorms were unusual in November, and this one finally seemed to be fading.

Thank you, Lord, for the rain and for always giving us enough food to eat. Bless those who are hungry and help us all to give from our hearts when we see people in need.

Chapter Ten

On Tuesday morning, Christopher asked Miss Luka if he could stay in from recess to count all the cans the class had collected so far.

"I suppose that would be all right," she said. "I have to go make some copies in the office during recess. Will you be all right in here alone?"

Christopher thought about it for a moment and then said, "Well, the counting might go faster if I had some help. Can Dylan stay in from recess too?"

He hadn't bothered to ask his friend if he'd mind missing recess, but since they always spent it together, he didn't think Dylan would mind. Christopher would have asked the teacher if Wyatt could help too, but he was home sick today.

Miss Luka hesitated a moment. "Can I trust you two to behave?"

Christopher gave her a solemn nod. "We'll be good, I promise."

She smiled. "That's what I like to hear."

When the recess bell rang, the rest of the sixth grade class filed neatly out the door, and then raced to the exit so they could beat the other students outside. Miss Luka watched them make it safely to the playground, and then she retrieved a file from her desk.

"I'll be in the office if you two need anything," she said.

"Okay," Dylan replied, shuffling over to Christopher's desk. "What are you working on?"

"A chart," he replied, carefully marking lines on the white poster board in front of him. "This will help us keep track of how many cans each class has at the end of each day. That way we'll know how we're doing in the competition."

He labeled the top of the chart with each class from kindergarten through sixth grade. Then he filled in the totals from Monday, which were pretty low across the board because a lot of students forgot about the food drive over the weekend.

Dylan frowned down at the numbers. "Looks like we're in third place. That's not good if we want to win."

"Kids brought a lot more cans today though," Christopher told him. "So we might be all right."

"Kids from other classes probably brought more cans too. I saw Mason Grover's mother carrying a huge box of cans into the kindergarten room this morning, and I heard her tell the kindergarten teacher she had another box in her car."

Christopher didn't like the sound of that. "Let's count our cans and see how many we have now."

They walked over to the corner where several boxes of cans were stacked together. They divided the boxes between them and began to count each can.

"I have sixty-three in my boxes," Christopher declared after several minutes.

Dylan held up a hand, his fingers twitching. "Hold on. I'm still counting."

"Do you want me to help?"

"No, you'll just mess me up."

Christopher waited, his eyes on the clock. Recess would be over soon, and he wanted to be done charting by then. "Hurry up."

"Hold your horses," Dylan said, and then resumed counting under his breath. "Fifty-one, fifty-two, fifty-three—okay, I have fifty-three." Then he wrinkled his nose. "Yuck, somebody brought a can of spinach. That stuff is terrible."

"Yeah, but at least whoever brought it doesn't have to eat it."

Dylan's eyes widened in approval. "I never thought of it that way. Maybe I'll go through our cupboards again and see what gross foods I can get rid of."

Christopher barely heard him as he bent over his chart to add up the numbers. "Okay, if we add the 35 cans that we had yesterday, then we have a total of 151 cans. Do you think that will be enough for our class to win?"

Dylan shrugged his narrow shoulders. "How should I know?"

Christopher really wanted to win the field trip. Plus, the more cans they donated, the more people they could help. He picked up the pencil off his desk and started adding up some numbers on a scrap of paper.

"Okay, the way I figure it, if all thirty students in our class brought five more cans, we'd be able to add 150 more cans to our total. If they each brought ten more cans, we could have three hundred."

"Wow," Dylan said. "That sounds like plenty to win."

Christopher agreed. When Miss Luka walked back into the classroom, he showed her his chart. "Can we put it up on the wall so everyone can see how we're doing?"

"I think that's an excellent idea," Miss Luka replied. She reached into her desk and brought out a roll of masking tape, handing it to Christopher.

"Why don't you hang it right by the door?" she suggested. "That will be a good way to remind the students when they leave for the day that they should bring cans the next morning."

"Could you make an announcement too?" Christopher asked her. "Dylan and I figured out a way to get a lot more cans for our class."

She peered at him over the top of her glasses. "You're the class leader on this project, Christopher. I think you should be the one to the make the announcement."

His stomach flip-flopped at the thought of talking in front of the entire class, but he knew that was his job. He exchanged a quick glance with Dylan, who gave him a thumbs-up.

"Okay," Christopher said at last. "I guess I can do it."

"Excellent." Miss Luka smiled at him. "I'll have you make the announcement as soon as the rest of the students return from recess."

He and Dylan walked over by the door to tape up the sign.

"I'm sure glad I'm not class leader," Dylan whispered to him.

Christopher was glad too, since the kids already teased Dylan a lot about his strange grunts and twitches. It would be hard enough for Christopher to stand at the front of the class, and he didn't have anything wrong with him.

As they finished taping the sign up, the bell rang signaling the end of recess. Soon the rest of their classmates piled back into the classroom.

Justin Taylor purposely bumped into Christopher on his way to his desk. Christopher stumbled, almost falling to the floor before he regained his balance. He looked over at the teacher, but she was writing on the whiteboard, unaware of what had just happened.

"Excuse you," Justin said rudely before continuing on his way.

Christopher ignored him, just like always. Nobody tangled with the class bully, especially since Justin had grown quite a bit between fifth and sixth grade. He was easily the tallest boy in the class and liked to throw his weight around.

After that, Christopher was even more reluctant to speak in front of the class. Justin would probably make faces at him when the teacher wasn't looking and the other kids would snicker along with him, just happy and relieved that Justin was picking on someone else.

"All right, class," Miss Luka said. "It's time to settle down. Before we begin our social studies lesson, Christopher would like to make an announcement about the food drive."

His cheeks flaming, Christopher rose up from his desk and walked to the front of the classroom. Turning to face his classmates, his first word still came out with a squeak. "We..."

Justin laughed until the teacher sent him a withering glance. Then he slumped down in his chair and scowled at Christopher as if he were to blame for Justin getting into trouble.

"Go on, Christopher," Miss Luka said, giving him an encouraging smile.

Christopher cleared his throat, and started over again, hoping he didn't squeak this time. "We are in third place right now in the food drive contest. If we want to win and go on a field trip to someplace really cool, then we have to bring a lot more cans."

"How many more?" Natalie Johnson asked.

"Well, if we each bring ten more cans, then that will be three hundred more cans added to the one hundred and fifty-one cans we already have. That's way more than any other class has right now."

"Let's do it!" one of the boys shouted from the back row.

Miss Luka put her index finger to her lips. "Not so loud, please."

"Okay, then," Christopher said, pleased by the excited faces in front of him. "Will everybody bring ten more cans this week?"

It looked to him like all the students nodded in agreement. "Great. Just think of the trip we'll get to take when we win."

As he walked back to his desk, he realized he was going to have to talk his grandma into donating more cans, and she'd already given him a lot. Still, she had said helping hungry people was living God's Word, so she probably wouldn't mind too much.

LATER THAT AFTERNOON, Charlotte and Emily sat at Dana's kitchen table poring over bridal magazines. Dana had invited them there after school, and Charlotte had brought a plate of fresh-baked chocolate chip cookies that now sat in the middle of the table.

"These wedding gowns are so lovely," Charlotte said, impressed by the beautiful designs and intricate beadwork.

"And *so* expensive," Dana replied, taking a second cookie off the plate. "I checked some of the prices online, and some of them cost *thousands* of dollars. That's a lot of money for a dress you only wear one day."

"But it's a big day," Emily countered, licking a smudge of chocolate off her finger. "Everyone will be looking at you."

Dana grimaced. "Don't remind me. Especially when I have a cookie in my hand. I should really lose a few pounds before the wedding."

Charlotte shook her head. "You look wonderful just the way you are. I was thin like you when I married Bob, so my dress would probably fit if you were a few inches shorter." Then she backtracked. "Not that you'd want to wear it, even if it did fit. After all, the style of my wedding gown is very outdated."

Dana smiled. "I'd love to wear your dress or my mom's wedding dress, but she says she doesn't even have hers anymore."

"I think you should have your own dress anyway," Emily told her. Then she pointed to a gown on the page. "Look at this one. I know it's expensive, but it's absolutely beautiful."

"It is," Dana agreed. "And absolutely out of my price

range. I think we should go to Bridal Images in Grand Island and check out those gowns. I've heard good things about that store. My mother could meet us all there."

"That sounds like fun," Charlotte said.

Dana turned to Emily. "You could bring Ashley if you want, so you don't have to hang around us old ladies all day."

Emily shrugged. "That's all right. I doubt Ashley would come anyway."

Dana glanced at Charlotte. "How come?"

"I'm not sure we're such close friends anymore."

"Oh, Emily," Charlotte admonished her, wondering if this was the reason her granddaughter had been moping around so much lately. "You know that's not true."

"It is true," Emily said, closing the magazine in front of her. "She never calls me anymore, and when I try to call her the phone is always busy because she's talking to Ryan."

"Ryan?" Dana echoed. "Ryan Holt?"

"Holt the dolt," Emily said. Then she caught the warning glance from her grandmother. "Okay, he's not really a dolt. I mean, he's smart, even if he does tell some really stupid jokes. I just wish . . ."

Her voice grew thick with tears, and Charlotte's heart went out to her. "You just wish what?"

She took a deep breath. "I just wish I had the old Ashley back. I really miss her."

Dana sat back in her chair, her expression thoughtful. "You know, I can remember the same thing happening to me when your mom started dating Kevin . . . your dad."

Emily looked up in surprise. "Really?"

Dana nodded. "We were really good friends, but Denise was crazy about him. It seemed like we just started growing apart. I mean, we were still friends, but it was just different."

Emily nodded. "That's how it is with me and Ashley."

"Just give it some time," Charlotte advised. "They just started dating. Sometimes these romances fizzle out pretty quickly, and you and Ashley could be right back where you were before."

Hope sparked in Emily's gray-green eyes. "Do you really think so?"

"It's certainly a good possibility," Charlotte told her. "In the meantime, why don't you start doing things with some of your other friends?"

Emily didn't look too thrilled with that idea. "I don't know. Ashley and I usually hang out together. It would be weird if I started calling other people to do things."

Dana leaned forward. "Is there anyone who likes to do the same things you do?"

Emily thought about the question for a long moment. "Hunter likes to ride horses. He even mentioned something about going riding together."

"Well, there you go," Dana said. "And he lives close by, so it would be easy for you to get together."

Charlotte feared it might be too easy. Still, Hunter seemed like a nice boy, and Emily had never shown any romantic interest in him.

"I'll think about it," Emily said, not quite ready to commit to anything. She grabbed another magazine. "Now let's look at the bridesmaids' dresses."

Chapter Eleven

On Saturday, Charlotte could hear father and son arguing before she even reached Pete's apartment door.

"I think you need another coat of paint," Bob shouted as Charlotte walked up the stairs of the tractor shed.

"It's my apartment, and I say one is plenty," Pete shouted back.

When she reached the door, Charlotte braced herself to play mediator again, just like she'd done yesterday when they'd argued about how to put up the wallpaper border in the bathroom.

Bob and Pete had been working on the apartment for most of the last week. The weather had been cool and overcast, leaving the fields wet longer than usual after a rain. In the last couple of days, the stress of waiting to resume farm work had started to take its toll, and both men were getting a little growly.

Charlotte inhaled the strong odor of paint as she stepped inside Pete's apartment. She liked the sage green color he'd painted the living room walls, although Bob had complained about that too.

"Who paints their walls green?" he'd said to her last night shortly after they'd gone to bed. "We see green every time we walk outdoors. Green grass, green pastures, green crops."

"Not in winter," she reminded him. "Besides, we've got white walls in our living room, and we see white every time we walk outside in the winter months."

He snorted. "I still say green is a crazy color to paint your walls."

Pete's apartment had had white walls ever since Ma Mildred had lived there. That seemed long enough to Charlotte, but Bob had a stubborn streak, as evidenced by his current argument with Pete.

"If I put on two coats I'm going to have to buy more paint," Pete explained to his father. "One coat will work just fine. Dana and I aren't going to live in this apartment forever."

Charlotte glanced at her husband, wondering if he'd ever thought about moving out of the house to let Pete move in. His parents had done that shortly after Bob and Charlotte were married.

A lot of retired farmers moved to town when the next generation took over the farm. Charlotte had even taken a drive or two along Bedford's streets and speculated about which house she'd choose if they moved there.

But that was before the grandkids had come to live with them. She certainly didn't want to uproot Sam, Emily, and Christopher again. They'd suffered enough upheaval in their lives after their mother died.

"Okay," Bob said, raising his arms in the air to signal his

surrender. "It's your apartment. Just don't say I didn't warn you."

"I won't," Pete promised. Then he turned to Charlotte. "Hey, Mom, come and take a look at the kitchen and tell me what you think."

She walked through the living room and was surprised to see the cheery gold walls in the kitchen. "I like it. The color really brightens the place up."

"Makes the cupboards look kind of dingy though," Pete said, folding his arms across his chest. "That might change once I put the new handles on."

"What are you going to do with the old handles?" Bob asked him. "You're not going to just throw them out, are you?"

"I don't need them," Pete replied. "You can have them if you want."

"I'll take 'em," Bob replied. "I don't believe in letting things go to waste."

Charlotte opened her mouth and then closed it again, wondering where her husband planned to store forty-year-old cupboard handles and drawer pulls. But, knowing Bob, he probably had a plan. She did admire the way he was able to recycle almost anything and put it to good use on the farm. It had saved them a lot of money over the years.

"I just came over to tell you I've got sandwiches made for lunch," Charlotte told them, "so come over to the house whenever you're ready to take a break."

"We're ready right now," Pete said, picking up a rag and wiping a spot of gold paint off his hands. "Can you wrap those sandwiches up for us while we get the combine and grain truck started?"

"You're harvesting today?" Charlotte asked, surprised by the news.

Bob nodded. "I checked the field a little while ago, and it's finally dry enough to drive the combine in without getting stuck."

Charlotte breathed a silent sigh of relief at the news. It would do them both good to get out of the tiny apartment for a while and back to the work they both loved. "I'll get right on it."

As she turned around and headed toward the door, Pete called her back.

"Hey, Mom, wait a minute."

Charlotte hesitated. "Yes?"

"I ordered some things online yesterday, so the UPS truck will probably be stopping by sometime in the next few days. Can you hold on to the packages for me if I'm not here?"

"What kind of things?" Bob asked. "For the apartment?"

Pete looked a little sheepish. "The more I fix up the place, the worse the old stuff looks. When I was surfing online yesterday I saw a couple of end tables I liked and a small dinette set."

Bob raked a hand through his hair. "You're going to spend yourself right into debt if you keep buying things like this. That's no way to start off a marriage."

"You let me worry about that."

Charlotte heard the edge in Pete's voice and knew it was time to intervene again. "You two better get going. I'll have those lunches packed and ready to go in just a few minutes."

Bob followed her out of the apartment, still muttering

about the expense of the renovations. "Pete's going to be a married man soon. He needs to learn how to save money instead of spend it."

"It's his money," Charlotte reminded Bob. "Besides, he's just trying to make the place nice for Dana."

"I thought it was plenty nice before all the changes."

Charlotte smiled to herself, knowing her husband didn't like change. But all of their lives would be changing when Pete brought his bride home to Heather Creek Farm.

WHAT AM I DOING HERE? Emily stood on the porch of the old Schnurnberger place trying to decide if she should knock on the door. She hadn't even planned on coming here when she'd saddled Princess to take her out for a ride, but somehow this is where she'd ended up.

In truth, she was just bored . . . and lonely. Ashley was off bowling with Ryan and his parents with no plans to get together with Emily this weekend. They'd talked briefly on the phone last night until Ryan had arrived to pick up Ashley for another date.

So now Emily had two choices. She could spend the weekend alone or she could take Hunter up on his offer to go riding together.

At least Princess seemed happy to be here. The sorrel filly was tied up to a wooden fencepost near the barn, grazing on the last remnants of green grass. Rambo, Hunter's quarter horse, stood watching her on the other side of the corral.

Before she could change her mind, Emily raised her fist

and knocked on the door. A few seconds later it opened and Hunter stood on the other side.

"Emily," he said, his dark eyes widening in surprise. "What are you doing here?"

"I was hoping you and Rambo would want to go out for a ride. Are you busy?"

"Yes," Hunter replied. "I mean no." He blushed. "I mean, I was just doing some homework, but that can wait for later."

"Are you sure?"

He grinned. "Am I sure I want to go riding instead of working on geometry problems? Yeah, I'm sure. Just hold on a minute."

She waited on the porch while Hunter shouted to his mother that he was going out for a ride. Then he joined her on the porch. "Let's go."

It didn't take him long to saddle Rambo, and soon they were both riding their horses down the long drive leading to the road.

"Where do you want to ride?" Emily asked, gently spurring her horse until she was riding alongside Hunter.

"There's a meadow about a mile from here. It's never been planted to anything but grass, so it's a nice place." Hunter shifted in the saddle. "I'm kinda surprised you came over today. You didn't seem very interested when I asked you before."

She smiled at him, enjoying the way she could make him blush just by looking at him. "Well, obviously I am interested or I wouldn't be here."

As soon as she said the words, his blush deepened. Emily

sensed Hunter might take them the wrong way, and she wondered if she should make it clear that she only wanted to be friends with him.

What does it matter? Emily thought to herself. *A little flirting never hurt anyone.* Besides, she'd been feeling like a third wheel ever since Ashley had started dating Ryan Holt. It was nice to be the center of attention for a change.

"So do you have any big plans for Thanksgiving?" Hunter asked as they ambled along the road. The fields to their left were almost picked clean.

"Not really. We're having Thanksgiving at our house and the whole family will be there, along with Miss Simons. She's marrying my uncle."

"That's probably a little weird to have him marrying one of your teachers..."

"Very weird, although I do really like her. Outside of school, she's like a regular person. She even wants my advice about her wedding gown and stuff."

"Cool." The sound of the horse hooves slapping against the pavement was the only noise for a moment, but then, to her surprise, Emily found herself telling Hunter everything about the wedding that she'd been wanting to tell Ashley. He was a good listener, although he didn't seem to know too much about dresses or the latest hairstyles.

"We're here," Hunter said at last, climbing down from his saddle to open the aluminum gate. He swung it wide enough for Emily to walk Princess through the entrance. Then he picked up Rambo's reins and followed Emily inside before closing the gate behind them.

Emily looked out over the meadow. The grass was turning brown, but it still stood knee-high and waved gently in the breeze. A few oak trees dotted the landscape, but not enough to hinder a good run.

Hunter grinned at her expression. "I thought you'd like it."

"I love it." She turned to look at him, and Hunter started blushing again. Emily tried to think of something to say that might interest him more than wedding fashions. "So . . . what are you doing for Thanksgiving?"

Hunter mounted Rambo, swinging his leg over the saddle in one easy movement.

"I think we're just getting together with some of my parents' friends in Harding for the day. Nothing too exciting." He studied the tip of his thumb as he continued speaking. "Maybe we could get together over Thanksgiving break and go riding or . . . something."

"That could be fun," Emily said, eager to let Princess have free rein in this wonderful, wide meadow. "Wanna race?"

Hunter looked over at her. "Sure." He pointed to the tree at the far end of the meadow. "First one to the tree wins."

Emily tightened her legs around the horse, and then leaned closer to Princess's neck. "Ready . . ."

Hunter tensed on his horse, his gaze on Emily. "Set . . ."

"Go!"

Chapter Twelve

"Welcome to our worship service this morning, and may God bless you all."

Charlotte sat in the pew with the rest of her family as Pastor Evans greeted the congregation. Christopher had squeezed in between her and Bob and now fidgeted nervously on the bench.

"What's wrong?" Charlotte whispered to her grandson.

"Nothing," Christopher whispered back, his eyes on Pastor Evans.

Charlotte wasn't convinced, but this wasn't the time or the place to get into a long discussion.

Pastor Evans shuffled some papers on the podium in front of him. "I'd like to begin with a few announcements. The Bible study group will meet in the fellowship hall tomorrow evening at seven o'clock to discuss the book of Isaiah..."

Charlotte listened to him list the church members on the prayer list and reminded herself to send get-well cards to those who were ill or facing surgery.

"Now," Pastor Evans said, "does anyone in the congregation have an announcement to make? Or perhaps a joy or concern they wish to share?"

To Charlotte's surprise, Christopher stood up and raised his hand in the air.

Bob turned to look at her. "What's he doing?" he mouthed.

"I don't know," she mouthed back, watching Pastor Evans smile as he pointed to Christopher.

"Yes, Christopher, do you have something to share with the congregation?"

"Well, sort of," Christopher said hesitantly. "It's not really a joy or a concern. I just wanted to tell everybody that my class is collecting canned goods for the food pantry, so if you want to donate something, you can give it to me or drop it off in the sixth-grade classroom at the school."

Pastor Evans chuckled. "Now, I would call that a joyful announcement. Anytime we can share our blessings with others is truly a joy."

Ten-year-old Trina Landrew shot out of her seat three rows ahead of the Stevenson family. "Pastor Evans, I have an announcement too."

"Go ahead, Trina."

She turned to look at the congregation. "My class is collecting food too, so you can give any cans that you want to donate to me or you can bring them to Miss Rivkin's fifth-grade class at the school."

Christopher scowled at her. Several members of the congregation began to chuckle as another child on the other side of the aisle stood up to make a similar announcement.

"I'm Sasha Corcoran, and I'm in second grade. We want to collect the most cans, so please bring them to my classroom at school."

"Well, now," Pastor Evans said, "I'm always happy to hear

that our youth members are working hard to serve others. If anyone would like to donate to the Bedford Elementary canned food drive, just take your cans to the school and I'm sure they can sort out where they should go."

Christopher stood up again. "No, see, we're having this contest, so it's very important that the cans go to the sixth grade . . ."

Charlotte grasped his arm and urged him back in his seat, shushing him at the same time.

Pastor Evans's face crinkled with amusement. "Dueling donations. That's an interesting concept. We may have to try it sometime."

Then he cleared his throat and grew serious again. "Now if everyone would please turn to page number 172 in their hymn book . . ."

"But Grandma," Christopher whispered, visibly upset, "I made the announcement first. They should bring the cans to my class."

"We'll talk about it later," Charlotte told him in a hushed voice as the organist began to play the introductory notes.

She thumbed through the pages in her hymnal, wondering how to get through to this child that the competition didn't matter as much as providing food for needy families. In part, she blamed the school for making it a contest, but she knew the administrators just wanted to collect as much food as possible for the pantry.

"Give thanks to the Lord," Pastor Evans proclaimed as the congregation rose to its feet, "for he is good. His love endures forever—Psalm 136:1."

Charlotte shared her hymnal with Christopher and they both began to sing a familiar hymn. The words and music soothed her ruffled nerves, and she looked over at Christopher, who sang in a small, sweet voice. He was a good boy and it was only natural he'd want to win the contest for his class since he'd been put in charge of the project.

And what was the harm in asking the congregation to donate to a good cause?

From the stern expression on Bob's face, Charlotte could see he didn't feel the same way about Christopher's unexpected announcement in church. He wasn't used to Christopher speaking up in public like that and, frankly, neither was she.

After the service was over, Christopher slipped out of the pew and hurried over to join some friends before either Charlotte or Bob had a chance to speak to him.

Dana's grandmother came up to her as they waited in line to greet the pastor.

"That Christopher sure is a cutie," Grandma Maxie said. "I like to see youngsters speak up in church. It means they feel like they're a real part of the church family."

Charlotte was glad Maxie wasn't offended and hoped the rest of the congregation felt the same way. She looked up to see her husband's reaction, but Bob was talking with Hank Richmond. At least he seemed more relaxed now that the service was over.

"Is Dana here?" Charlotte asked, realizing she hadn't seen her yet.

Maxie shook her head. "I'm afraid she woke up with a sore throat this morning and decided to stay home."

"That was probably a wise decision. Pete's been complaining of a sore throat too, but I thought it was from all the . . ."

She was about to say *paint*, but then remembered that the apartment renovations were supposed to be a secret. Pete probably wouldn't care if she told Maxie, but she'd promised not to say anything to anyone.

"From the what?" Maxie prodded.

"From all the dust that gets kicked up during harvest," Charlotte replied.

That was true and probably a more likely explanation than the paint fumes. Still, she felt a little uneasy not being completely open with Maxie and intended to ask Pete if he'd mind if she let Dana's grandma in on the secret.

"Well, I hope he feels better soon." She reached out to give Charlotte's hand a warm squeeze. "I just want to tell you how happy we are to welcome Pete into our family. We were beginning to worry that Dana would never find the right man."

Charlotte smiled, realizing everyone worried about their children and grandchildren, no matter what their age. "We're so thrilled about their engagement," she replied, "and we can't wait to welcome Dana to Heather Creek Farm."

Maxie chuckled. "Farm life will be an adjustment for her, I'm sure, but I think she'll grow to love it."

"I know I did."

They reached Pastor Evans, and he greeted Charlotte with a wide smile. "There's the proud grandmother. I must say I was surprised to see Christopher make an announcement today. I've hardly heard him string more than a sentence or two together since he moved here."

"I guess he's starting to feel more comfortable here."

"I'll say he is," Pastor Evans replied. "Tell him that I commend him for asking people to help and to keep up the good work."

"I will," Charlotte promised, moving toward the door. She hoped the pastor's words would ease Bob's displeasure at Christopher's actions.

"I'll see you later, Charlotte," Maxie said, pulling her jacket closer as they stepped outside into the cool November air.

"Take care, Maxie."

Charlotte looked around for the rest of the family, not sure how they'd all gotten separated. She spotted Sam and Christopher by the car with Bob, but there was no sign of Emily.

She went looking for her, knowing Bob would grow impatient as dinnertime approached. His diabetes made eating on schedule important so she didn't want to make him wait too long.

As she rounded the corner of the church, she ran into Nicole Evans, the pastor's daughter, who was talking with her friend Lily.

"Hello, Mrs. Stevenson," Nicole said sweetly. "Are you looking for Emily?"

"Yes, I am," Charlotte said, curious at the impish gleam in Nicole's eyes.

Lily pointed behind her. "She's at the back of the church."

"Thank you," Charlotte said, taking off in that direction.

"You better hurry," Nicole called after her. "They didn't look too happy with each other."

She had no idea what Nicole's cryptic words meant. "Oh, Lord, give me patience with that girl," she murmured to herself.

Unfortunately, Nicole's meaning became all too clear when Charlotte reached the back parking lot of the church and saw Emily and Ashley engaged in a very heated discussion.

"So you expect me to just sit around by myself waiting for you to call?" Emily shouted. "Do you really think I have nothing better to do?"

Ashley stared at her in surprise. "What's gotten into you? I just asked why you weren't home when I called last night and you go all ballistic on me."

"I didn't go ballistic. I just don't like the way you're treating me."

Irritation flashed across Ashley's face. "The way *I'm* treating *you*? You're the one who's shouting, and I don't even know why."

Charlotte hesitated, not certain if she should interfere or simply let them have it out. At least the parking lot was mostly empty by now, so the girls weren't drawing a crowd.

"Because you just make me so mad sometimes." Emily inhaled a deep, shuddering breath, and then lowered her voice. "For your information, I was having dinner with Hunter and his family last night. That's why I wasn't home when you called."

Ashley stepped back in surprise. "Hunter Norris? Have you been hanging around with him?"

"Why would you care? You haven't asked one thing about me or my life since you started going out with your new boyfriend."

Ashley folded her arms across her chest. "Is that what this is about? Why don't you like Ryan? He's a perfectly nice guy."

"This isn't about Ryan," Emily said, her voice thick with tears now.

"Then why are you so upset with me?" Ashley asked, sounding completely perplexed. "I don't even know what we're fighting about."

Emily tipped up her chin. "Well, if you don't know, then I'm not going to tell you."

Charlotte heard a giggle behind her, and she turned around to see Nicole and Lily spying on the two girls from behind an evergreen bush.

"Emily," Charlotte said evenly, ready to end the show, "it's time to go."

At the sound of her grandmother's voice, Emily's tears overflowed, and she ran toward the direction of Bob's truck.

Ashley turned to Charlotte. "Mrs. Stevenson, what's wrong with Emily? I don't get why she's so upset with me. What did I do?"

Charlotte moved closer to the girl, determined to keep their conversation private. She reached out to pat Ashley's arm, aware that she was on the verge of crying as well.

"It's hard to explain," Charlotte began, knowing the two girls needed to find a way to work it out between themselves. "Why don't you give Emily a call later today and try to talk about it some more?"

"Okay," Ashley said helplessly. "I guess I will. I just hope she wants to talk to me."

Charlotte watched Ashley leave, and then followed Emily

to the car. Bob and the boys were sitting inside with the driver's window cracked open, listening to the radio. Her granddaughter stood by the back bumper, wiping the tears off her face.

"Are you all right?" Charlotte asked her.

"Yes," Emily said, sniffing a little. "I just don't want Grandpa or Sam or Christopher to see me crying. Do I look all right?"

Charlotte gazed into Emily's watery gray-green eyes. "Your eyes are a little red, but I don't think Grandpa or the boys will notice."

"Good," Emily said with a final sniff.

"I think Ashley's planning to call you later."

Emily's expression hardened. "Well, I won't be home. I'm going riding with Hunter this afternoon."

"Again?" Charlotte shifted uneasily on her feet, her black pumps pinching her toes. "You just went riding with Hunter yesterday and spent most of the evening at his house."

"Well, he asked me to go riding with him today and I didn't have anything else to do so I said yes." She cocked her head in Charlotte's direction. "Is that okay with you, Grandma?"

Charlotte thought about it for a moment, and then nodded. After all, she was the one who had encouraged Emily to seek out other friends. "Just be careful. I think Hunter likes you, and we don't want him to get hurt."

"Don't worry," Emily assured her. "I've got everything under control."

Chapter Thirteen

"Sam, are you ready?" Charlotte heard the sound of a car on the road and walked into the kitchen to look out the window. A flash of headlights briefly illuminated the window pane as the car turned into the driveway. "Jake and his parents are here."

"Be right down," Sam called from his bedroom.

She hurried to the hall closet to retrieve Sam's winter coat. It was only in the high thirties right now, and she wasn't about to let him go all the way to Lincoln without a warm coat to wear.

Sam bounded down the stairs, more chipper than usual at six thirty in the morning. That was probably due to the fact that he got to skip school today to go on his college tours.

"Do you have everything?" Charlotte asked, handing him his coat and following him into the kitchen. "Money? Your registration papers for Red Letter Day? Coach Tucker's phone number?"

"Yeah, I have everything I need," Sam said, slipping on his coat. "I'll give you the full report when I get home tonight."

"All right," she said, walking him to the door. "Have a good time and be careful. Be sure and mind Mr. and Mrs. Perkins."

"I will," he promised.

"And offer to chip in some gas money," Charlotte reminded him. Bob had handed over some cash to Sam last night for just that purpose.

"Will do." Sam opened the back door, letting in a blast of cold air. "Bye, Grandma."

"Bye, Sam."

She closed the door behind him, and then watched out the window as he climbed into Jake's parents' Volvo. There was a strange ache inside of her, even though she knew he'd be back tonight. This was the first step in his going off on his own and leaving Heather Creek Farm.

"Did Sam leave already?" Bob asked as he walked into the kitchen.

"They just pulled out of the driveway and are on their way to Lincoln."

She dropped the curtain and walked over to the counter to pour Bob a cup of coffee. "Would you like some eggs this morning?"

"Sounds good. Pete wants to get an early start on the corn today."

"The sun's not even up yet."

Bob sat down at the table and rubbed his jaw. "I know it. That boy is in a big hurry to get back to work on his apartment."

Charlotte set the steaming coffee cup in front of him, opened the refrigerator, and pulled out a bowl of eggs. "He seems pretty excited about all the improvements he's making."

"It's not looking too bad," Bob admitted, blowing gently on his coffee. "I still don't like the green walls though."

Charlotte smiled to herself as she added a drop of oil to the frying pan on the stove and then cracked an egg against the side.

"Are Emily and Christopher up yet?"

The first egg began to sizzle as she cracked the second and dropped it into the pan. "Emily's in the shower, and I'm letting Christopher sleep until seven. He was pretty tuckered out last night."

"He's really taking this food drive business seriously, isn't he?"

"It seems pretty important to him."

"Important enough to pipe up in church," Bob muttered. "I hope you talked to him about that."

"I doubt he'll do it again," Charlotte said as she flipped both eggs over. Bob liked them over easy, so she only let them cook for a few more seconds before she scooped them up with her spatula and slid them onto his plate.

"Here you go," she said, setting the plate in front of him.

He looked up at her. "Aren't you having any eggs?"

"I'm not really hungry." She sat down in the chair across from him. "I think it's because I'm worried about Emily."

"You worry about the kids too much," he said, reaching for the salt and pepper shakers.

"I told you about the fight she and Ashley had yesterday. Well, Ashley tried to call her last night, but Emily just isn't ready to make up yet. I'm afraid if she waits too long, she may lose a good friend."

"It's only been a day," Bob told her. "Give it some time."

She sighed. "I suppose you're right."

"If you want something to worry about, it's how we're going to be able to afford to send Sam to college. I read an article in the newspaper yesterday that all the Nebraska colleges are increasing their tuition." He shook his head. "I don't know how we're going to do it, Charlotte. I just don't know. Especially with Emily following him in just two more years. There's the money from the video shoot with Shae Lynne, but that will only go so far."

Charlotte believed God would provide, but times in general were getting tougher. "Maybe Sam will get a scholarship offer. Then we won't have to foot the entire college bill."

"That may be his only hope."

"KNOCK, KNOCK."

Hannah cracked open the back door. "Anybody home?"

"Come on in," Charlotte said, rising up from the table. She'd been reading her devotional since Sam's early departure for Lincoln. Bob's eagerness to get to the field hadn't left her enough time to do it before breakfast.

"Looks like you're busy," Hannah said as she walked inside. She carried a large box in her hands. "I don't want to bother you."

"I'm not busy at all. I could use some company, actually. The house always seems so quiet after the kids leave for school."

"Well, I won't keep you long. Frank and I are visiting his sister this afternoon, and I wanted to drop this by before we left."

"What is it?" Charlotte asked as Hannah opened the lid.

"Cans for Christopher," Hannah replied. "A bunch of ladies at church said they wanted to donate to the food drive, so I volunteered to bring them out here."

Charlotte was touched by their generosity. "That was nice of you."

Hannah laughed. "I sure didn't want to take them to the school and try to figure out which cans should go to which classrooms. I heard other people talking about donating to Trina and Sasha though, so there should be plenty of canned goods to go around."

"I'm sure Christopher will be thrilled to see what you've brought him." Charlotte took the heavy box from her and set it on the counter. "Although, to tell you the truth, I'll be glad when this canned food drive is over."

"Is the competition getting to you, Grandma?"

Charlotte sighed. "I'm not sure if it's the competition or the fact that Christopher seems more focused on winning than giving. I know that's not unusual for a boy his age, but it still bothers me."

"Well, I don't think you should worry too much about it." She chuckled. "I remember an episode of *The Brady Bunch* where Cindy and Bobby were competing for the school quiz bowl team. Cindy beat him out and was pretty proud of herself while Bobby was hoping she'd fall on her face during the televised competition."

"So what happened?"

"She did fall on her face, figuratively, that is. Froze up when she saw the television camera and couldn't answer a single question. 'Course, then Bobby felt bad for hoping she'd fail."

"So they both learned something," Charlotte surmised.

Hannah nodded her head. "Whether he wins or loses that contest, I'm sure Christopher will learn something from it too. Besides, the boy's got a good head on his shoulders. I'm sure he'll be all right."

"I hope so."

Charlotte was tempted to confide her worries about Sam and Emily as well, but she knew Hannah couldn't stay long, and she didn't want to delay her trip to visit Frank's sister.

"You let me know if Christopher needs more cans," Hannah said as Charlotte walked her to the door. "I'll scrounge some up somewhere."

"I will," Charlotte promised, and then saw a car turn into the driveway. "Well, this is a surprise."

"You've just got all kinds of visitors today." Hannah said. "It looks like Anna."

"It is," she said, waving to Bill's wife. "I didn't realize she was coming."

Hannah waved to her too, before heading for her car. Charlotte waited by the door while Anna slowly made her way to the house.

"Hello, Charlotte." She laid a hand on her protruding middle. "Sorry to make you stand in the cold for so long. I'm not moving too fast these days."

"That's all right." Charlotte said, holding the door open for her. "You look wonderful. Only a few more weeks, and that baby boy will finally be here."

"I know. The girls are so excited for their little brother they can hardly wait."

Charlotte smiled at her pregnant daughter-in-law. "I feel exactly the same way."

Anna walked over to the table and pulled out a chair. "Hope you don't mind if I sit down. My back's been bothering me lately. The obstetrician gave me some stretching exercises to do but they don't seem to help much."

"The last month is always the most uncomfortable," Charlotte said, remembering her own pregnancies. "But it will all be worth it."

"Oh, I know." Anna looked around the kitchen. "I thought Bob might be here to help me load up."

"Load up?" Charlotte echoed. Then it clicked. "Oh, are you here for your baby furniture?"

Anna stared at her in dismay. "Didn't Bill call you yesterday to tell you I'd be coming?"

Charlotte shook her head. "No, he didn't. He did mention something about picking up the furniture sometime when I talked to him a couple of weeks ago."

Anna sighed. "I knew I should have called here myself. We finally finished turning that little office into a nursery, and I just want everything set up in there before the baby arrives."

"That's understandable," Charlotte was tempted to offer to carry down the furniture herself, but she'd suffered her own back injury a few months ago and didn't want to risk hurting it again. "So you decided not to add on to the house?"

"We're going to hold off for a while," Anna replied. "Poor Bill has been so busy, both at his office and taking care of everything at home. I just hate the fact that I made the trip here for nothing."

Charlotte decided not to take the remark personally.

"Don't worry. Bob usually stops in here about midmorning for a snack to help to keep his blood sugar under control. He can load the furniture for you then."

"Good," Anna said with a sigh of relief.

"We can just sit in the living room and have a nice visit while we wait for Bob. Would you like some milk and cookies?"

Anna placed her hand on her stomach. "Thank you for the offer, but I've been feeling a little queasy since I got up this morning. I think I'll just have a glass of ice water."

"Coming up," Charlotte said, filling a glass for her before they headed out of the kitchen.

"How are Jennifer and Madison?" Charlotte asked as they walked down the hallway.

"They're good as gold," Anna began, and then paled as she reached out to brace herself against the wall.

Alarmed, Charlotte moved closer to her. "Anna, are you all right?"

"I don't know," Anna breathed, her eyes wide with alarm. "I felt a strange . . . twinge. It almost felt like a contraction."

Chapter Fourteen

"You need to lie down."

Charlotte tried not to show her concern as she gently led Anna to the living room sofa. She helped her ease down onto the cushions, and then propped a pillow under Anna's head.

"Are you cold?"

"A little," Anna said. "I might just be scared though. It's too early for the baby."

Charlotte grabbed a quilted throw and tucked it around Anna. "There's no reason to be scared. Are you sure it was a contraction?"

She hesitated. "I don't know. It started at my back and sort of traveled around to my stomach. It didn't last long though, only a second or two."

"Have you had one since then?"

Anna shook her head. "I'm probably fine. I just haven't been feeling well, and the drive here from River Bend seemed so long. I drove my dad's SUV so I could fit all the furniture inside, but it sure isn't very comfortable—especially when you're eight months pregnant."

"I'm sure it isn't." Charlotte felt Anna's forehead. She might be coming down with a stomach virus. "You don't have a fever. Do you want me to call Bill or your doctor?"

She shook her head. "Just let me rest here for a little bit. Those bumpy country roads probably just jarred me a bit."

Charlotte didn't want Anna to feel like she was hovering over her so she walked over to the rocking chair and took a seat.

A long, awkward silence stretched between them. Charlotte had never warmed up to Bill's wife as much as she would have liked. Anna's penchant for blunt honesty had caused some hurt feelings in the past, and Charlotte had never felt it was easy to talk to her.

Still, she was family, and Charlotte said a prayer for her. Anna's face was pale, and she had dark circles under her eyes.

"Why are you staring at me?" Anna asked. "Do I look that bad?"

"No," Charlotte said slowly. "I'm just concerned."

Anna struggled to sit up. "Well, I think it was a false alarm. I haven't had even the slightest twinge since that first one."

"I'm not sure I want you driving in your condition. Why don't you call Bill to come and get you? Or I could even drive you home and Bob could come and pick me up in River Bend."

Charlotte knew Bob wouldn't be too thrilled with that plan since he was helping Pete in the fields, but family always came first for both of them.

"Not necessary," Anna said crisply. "I really should . . ." Her voice trailed off as her face contorted. "Ahhhh!"

Charlotte rushed to her side as Anna doubled over in pain. "Hold on to me."

Anna grabbed her arms until the contraction passed. "It's too early! The baby can't be coming yet."

"I'm going to call the ambulance."

"No," Anna said, still hanging on to her. "Can you take me to the medical center in Bedford? I don't want to be poked and prodded by some volunteer EMTs who don't know what they're doing."

Charlotte would have argued with her, but she knew they could probably drive to town faster than it would take the ambulance to get here. "Okay, let's walk slowly to your car. It's closer than mine and bigger, so it will probably be easier to fit into."

Anna didn't argue with her. Tears shone in her eyes. "The baby can't be coming yet. It just can't."

Please, Lord, help us. Be with Anna and this baby. Please don't let anything happen to either one of them. Charlotte prayed all the way to the medical center.

She drove the SUV right up to the emergency doors and then rang the buzzer for help before hurrying over to the passenger side of the SUV to help Anna out. Kelley Flynn, an RN, and two aides came rushing outside, one of them pushing a wheelchair. Charlotte stood back as they helped Anna into it, her heart beating a mile a minute.

"You'll need to move your car, Charlotte." Kelley, whom Charlotte had seen many times when she'd gone to the medical center for various appointments, gave her a reassuring smile. "Don't worry. We'll take good care of her. Just park the car in the lot and come right back inside."

Charlotte nodded, not trusting herself to speak yet.

She climbed back into the SUV and carefully drove it into the parking lot, her hands shaking now. She'd been steady as a rock until the hospital workers took over. Now she felt like she was about to fall apart.

After she'd parked the car and turned off the ignition, she folded her hands together and bowed her head over the steering wheel. "Heavenly Father, please give me strength and help me be a comfort to Anna. Be with the hospital workers, Lord, and help them keep the baby safe and healthy. Amen."

She took a moment to gather herself, before climbing out of the SUV and heading into the medical center.

The receptionist met her at the door and asked for information about Anna. Charlotte told her everything she knew: Anna's name, address, doctor's name, and how far along she was in her pregnancy. She wasn't able to answer questions about insurance or any medications Anna was taking.

"I need to call her husband," Charlotte said, moving toward the reception counter. She should have done that as soon as they left the house. "Can I use your phone?"

"Of course."

Charlotte picked up the receiver, but then hesitated. She didn't know Bill's cell phone number from memory, but she could recall his office number. It rang six times before someone finally picked up.

"Stevenson Law Office, how may I help you?"

Charlotte recognized the voice of his secretary. "Hello, Lena, this is Bill's mother, Charlotte. Is he there?"

"Oh, hello, Charlotte," Lena said. "I haven't seen you in a while. How are you?"

Lena was a sweet woman, but she did not have the best secretarial skills. Charlotte took a deep breath. "I'm fine, Lena, but I need to speak to Bill right away. It's an emergency."

"Oh, no, what's the matter?"

"It's a medical emergency. Please just put me through to Bill."

"Oh, of course," Lena said, her voice filled with concern. "Right away. Just hang on."

A moment later, Bill's voice sounded over the line. "Mom? What's wrong? Is it Dad?"

She took another deep breath, telling herself the last thing she wanted to do was send Bill into a panic. "It's Anna. She had a couple of contractions at the farm and . . ."

"Anna?" he interjected, sounding perplexed. Then he groaned. "Oh, no. She was making a trip to the farm today, wasn't she? I completely forgot. I was supposed to call you . . ."

"I know," Charlotte replied. "She made it to the farm just fine, but she wasn't feeling well. She just had a twinge at first, and then a much stronger contraction."

"Did you call her doctor?" Bill's voice was filled with concern.

"We're at the Bedford Medical Center and they're attending to her now. We just got here a few minutes ago."

"I'm on my way."

A dial tone sounded in Charlotte's ear, and she hung up the phone. Poor Bill sounded so worried. She just hoped he'd be careful driving to Bedford.

As Kelley came out of the examining room, Charlotte stood up and hurried to her. "Can I see Anna?"

"I'm afraid not," she replied. "The doctor is examining her now, but I'll let you know as soon as you can see her."

"And the baby?" Charlotte asked. "Is he all right?"

"I'm sorry," Kelley said gently. "I really can't tell you anything more at this point."

Charlotte paced the gray linoleum floor, too worried to sit down and wait. After several minutes, she tried calling the farm, but there was no answer. Bob had probably retrieved his snack from the kitchen and was already back on Jimmy's Quarter, harvesting with Pete.

Sam was in Lincoln, or else she might have called the school and had him drive out to the farm to get Pete and Bob—not that there was anything they could do—and the last thing Anna would probably want would be a big crowd gathering here waiting to see her.

She paced some more, wishing Hannah were home. Then she thought of someone to call. She walked over to the reception desk and called the church office to ask Pastor Evans to come to the medical center.

"I'm sorry, Pastor Evans isn't in the office," Karen Ellis, the church secretary, told her. A retired air force lieutenant who still wore her gray hair cut very short, the woman kept the church office in tip-top shape. "He's making hospital calls in Harding and Grand Island today."

"Oh, all right," Charlotte replied with a twinge of disappointment. "Please let him know I'd appreciate prayers for my daughter-in-law, Anna. She's having some problems with her pregnancy."

"I will," Karen promised. "And I'll be praying for her too, Charlotte."

"Thank you, Karen. I appreciate it."

After Charlotte hung up the phone, she continued to pace and pray in the waiting room, worrying about what might be happening inside that exam room. How would she ever explain it to the grandkids if something happened to the baby? They'd already experienced too much loss in their young lives.

"Stop it," Charlotte told herself. "Trust in the Lord and stop thinking the worst."

After what seemed like hours, but was really only about twenty minutes, Bill came running through the doors of the medical center.

"Mom!" he called, spotting her in the waiting room. "Where is she?"

She rushed over to meet him. "Still with the doctor. The nurse said he'll be out here to talk to us soon."

He nodded, trying to remain calm, but she could see the tension in his jaw and the way his hair stood up told her he'd been running his hand through it all the way from River Bend.

"Why don't you sit down?" she said, giving advice she wasn't able to take herself.

"No," he said, looking over at the closed exam room door. "I can't sit still. I never should have let Anna go to the farm by herself to pick up the baby furniture. It's just that I've been so busy." He shook his head. "It's my fault."

"It's no one's fault," Charlotte said. "I'm sure Anna will be fine. She's in good hands with Dr. Carr. She just needs you to stay calm."

"You're right." Bill took a deep breath, and then gave Charlotte a hug. "I'm just so glad you were there to help her. If this had happened while she was on the road . . ."

"It didn't," Charlotte told him, refusing to let him imagine worst-case scenarios. "She only had two contractions, and we came straight here after the second one."

He nodded. "Okay. So she might be in labor, but we don't know for sure. Dr. Carr is in with her and I'm sure if it's serious, he'll send her on to Harding."

"That's right," Charlotte said, watching her son take stock of the situation.

Bill was always good at assessing a situation before taking action, and doing so now seemed to help calm him down.

The door to the exam room opened and Dr. Carr walked out. Bill and Charlotte hurried over to him.

"How's Anna?" Bill asked.

"She's fine," Dr. Carr assured him. "So is the baby. His heartbeat is strong and the contractions have finally stopped."

"Thank you, God," Charlotte said, emotion welling up in her throat.

Bill closed his eyes for a moment, relief washing over his face. Then he opened them again. "Can I see her?"

Dr. Carr nodded. "In a minute. I just want to go over what happened and tell you what I told her."

"Of course," Bill said, gathering himself once more.

"Anna did experience some mild contractions," Dr. Carr explained. "Fortunately, they grew weaker shortly after she arrived."

"Do you know what caused it?"

"A combination of things," Dr. Carr explained. "Her chronic back pain has put stress on her body, and she's just been trying to do too much. She needs bed rest immediately and lots of it. Of course, you should check with her OB once she's home to make sure he or she concurs with my opinion."

"We'll do that," Bill said. "Can I take her home today? Will it be safe for her to travel?"

"I want to keep her here for another hour or so just for monitoring, but she's going to be just fine."

Chapter Fifteen

"I'm home."

Charlotte opened her eyes at the sound of Sam's voice. She'd been dozing on the sofa, the baby quilt she'd been working on still in her lap. She straightened up, stretching her neck and shoulders to get the kinks out. "I must have fallen asleep."

"Yep," Bob said from behind the newspaper. "Guess all the excitement at the hospital wore you out."

"What excitement?" Sam asked as he walked into the family room.

Charlotte carefully folded the quilt and set it aside. "Anna stopped by earlier today and started having contractions, so I took her to the medical center. The doctor ordered bed rest for the next few weeks, but he told us both the baby and Anna are healthy."

Sam slipped off his jacket and tossed it on a chair. "Well, that's good that she's okay. Where are Emily and Christopher?"

"Upstairs doing homework," Charlotte replied.

"And Pete's peeling up the linoleum on his kitchen floor, if you're looking for something to do," Bob told him, closing the newspaper.

Sam shook his head. "I'm beat. It was a really long day."

With all the drama of Anna's crisis, Charlotte had given little thought to Sam's college tours. Now she wanted to hear all about them. "So how was Lincoln? Tell us everything."

"There's not all that much to tell." He plopped down on the other end of the sofa. "We started at the University of Nebraska-Lincoln first. There were lots of other high school seniors there checking the place out. I mean, literally hundreds."

Charlotte wanted to know about his meeting with Coach Tucker at Wesleyan, but she decided to let Sam tell the story at his own pace.

"We all sat in this big auditorium first and heard some boring speeches by campus bigwigs. Then we split up into groups and took a tour of the campus."

"How did you like it?" Bob asked. "Was it too big for you?"

Sam shook his head. "Looked just about right to me. Lots of things to do and our guide said it has one of the best recreation centers for college students in the country. They even have this indoor field that kids can use to play soccer or flag football."

"What about the classrooms?" Charlotte asked him, hoping Sam realized the main purpose of attending college was academics, not athletics.

"They were okay," he replied. "Some were modern and high tech, and others were in buildings that had to be at least a hundred years old. I mean, the desks and furniture were fine, but the buildings themselves were ancient. The guide seemed really proud of the old stuff."

Charlotte smiled at his description. For someone who

claimed there wasn't much to tell about his trip, Sam certainly was providing a lot of details.

"What else did you do?" Bob asked him.

"We ate lunch at one of the dorm cafeterias, and the food was actually pretty decent. They have, like, five cafeterias on campus and the menus are all different, so there's lots of variety."

Charlotte's smile widened. She had a feeling that sports and food were probably going to have a big influence on his choice of college. Still, it seemed like he was impressed with the facilities over all. She knew the university had grown a lot recently, but she hadn't actually been on the campus since Bill's law school graduation.

"Oh, and I met with an academic adviser," Sam said, almost as an afterthought. "He asked me what kind of classes I liked in high school and if I knew what I wanted to major in."

Bob folded the newspaper in half and set it on the floor beside his recliner. "What did you tell him?"

"I told him I didn't really like any of my classes and I had no idea what I wanted to major in."

Bob snorted. "Well, I guess that's the truth anyway."

"Yeah, it seemed like he'd heard it before because he just smiled when I said it." Sam stretched out his legs. "Then he told me that a lot of kids don't know what they want to do when they first come to college, so they're considered 'undeclared,' or they major in something like general studies."

"What about Nebraska Wesleyan?" Charlotte asked, trying not to appear too eager. "Did you meet with the soccer coach?"

"Yeah, I did." Sam shrugged. "He seemed like a cool guy."

"Does he want you on the team?" Bob asked him.

Sam nodded. "The good news is that he said there's a spot for me if I'm interested. The bad news is that Nebraska Wesleyan doesn't offer athletic scholarships for any of their sports."

Charlotte's heart sank, and at that moment she realized how much her hopes had been pinned on Sam getting a scholarship there. "Why not?"

He shrugged. "The coach just said that sports isn't their main focus and as a small, private college they've got limited funds to pass around."

Sam tried to sound nonchalant, but Charlotte could see the disappointment etched in his face.

"Well, there goes that plan," Bob said, irritated. "The coach could have told you that before you made a special trip to Lincoln to meet with him."

"Jake was going anyway," Sam countered, "and maybe it was a good thing, because now I'm wondering if I even want to go to college."

"Oh, Sam!" Charlotte exclaimed. "Please don't say that."

"I mean it, Grandma. Both campuses are cool and the students look like they're having fun, but I have no idea what I want to do with my life and no money to pay for college. Maybe I should just work full-time for a couple of years after high school, and then decide what I want to do."

"Might not be a bad idea," Bob said.

She shot a warning look at her husband, not wanting him to encourage that kind of talk when Sam seemed so dejected. She knew Denise would want Sam to go to college, and

Charlotte feared that if Sam put it off he might never get there.

"Uncle Pete never went to college," Sam continued. "Neither did my mom or dad."

"College isn't for everyone," Charlotte said slowly. "But I don't think you should give up so easily until you've given it more thought and visited more colleges. There are technical schools too, and community colleges. The one in Harding has several good programs. So does the one in Grand Island."

Sam shrugged. "Nothing sounds good to me right now."

"Well, you don't have to decide anything tonight," she told him. "In fact, you've got the rest of your senior year to make a decision."

Sam looked up at her. "Arielle and the kids at school are already applying to colleges. The guidance counselor said we shouldn't wait too long."

"You can apply to several schools," Charlotte said. "You could see where you get in and then make a decision."

Bob frowned. "Isn't there an application fee each time he applies?"

"Yes, but we can cover that," she said firmly. "It's more important that Sam get admitted into the college he wants to go to than it is to save a few dollars here and there."

Bob opened his mouth to disagree with her, but then he apparently saw the expression on Charlotte's face and thought better of it. "Well, we can talk about it later."

"Yeah," Sam said, rising to his feet, "I'm tired. I think I'll go up to my room and hit the books. I want to go to bed early tonight."

Charlotte waited until Sam had left the room and then

turned to Bob. "I wish that coach at Nebraska Wesleyan could have offered him a soccer scholarship. He sounds so disappointed."

Bob reached down for the newspaper. "Well, maybe it's for the best. He's got no idea what he wants to do with his life. Why go to college until he knows?"

Charlotte realized he had a point and that college wasn't necessary for everyone. She'd never gone herself and neither had Bob, but times were different now. She wanted her grandchildren to have the best opportunities possible.

"Besides," Bob continued, turning to the agricultural section of the newspaper, "if he still wanted to go to Nebraska Wesleyan to play soccer how would we pay for it? We have to be realistic, Charlotte."

She didn't have an answer for him, so she decided to take what action she could to make Sam feel better. "I'm going to make Sam a snack. I'm sure he's hungry after such a long trip."

"Okay," Bob murmured, already engrossed in one of the articles.

Bob's question still reverberated in Charlotte's mind as she climbed the stairs with a plate in one hand and a glass in the other.

The phone rang as she reached the top of the stairs.

"I'll get it," Christopher shouted, running out of his room and into the spare bedroom, where he picked up the extension. "Hello?"

Charlotte waited there to see if it was for her. She'd been hoping Bill would call and let them know how Anna was doing. She didn't want to call in case her daughter-in-law was sleeping.

"Emily," Christopher called out, placing his hand over the bottom of the receiver, "it's for you."

Charlotte moved toward Sam's room, still able to see Christopher through the open door of the spare bedroom. She hoped it was Ashley calling and that the two of them could make up.

Emily appeared in the doorway of her bedroom. She looked straight ahead at her little brother, unaware that Charlotte was standing there. "Who is it?"

"Hunter."

She groaned. "I just talked to him a few hours ago. Tell him I'm busy."

"Busy doing what?" Christopher prodded.

"I don't know," she replied, annoyed. "Tell him I'm in the shower or washing my hair."

Christopher shrugged as he turned back to the phone. "Okay."

Charlotte pressed her lips together, not liking what she'd just heard. Emily disappeared back into her bedroom and closed the door while Christopher gave Hunter the excuse that she was in the shower.

Charlotte turned around and knocked on Sam's door.

"Come in."

Resting the plate in the crook of her arm, she opened the door. "I brought you something to eat."

Sam sat on his bed, his history book lying open in front of him. "Hey, thanks, Grandma. We grabbed supper in York, but I'm still kind of hungry."

She set the sandwich and milk on his nightstand. "Is there anything else you want?"

He shook his head. "No, I'm good."

Charlotte left his room and made a beeline for Emily's door.

She knocked, and then placed her hand on the doorknob. "Come in," Emily called.

Charlotte walked inside to find her granddaughter standing in front of her closet looking at her clothes. "What are you doing?"

"Trying to decide what to wear tomorrow."

Charlotte placed her hands on her hips. "And that was more important than talking to Hunter? I heard what you told Christopher to tell Hunter when he called here for you."

Emily turned to face her. "I just didn't feel like talking. It's no big deal."

Charlotte reached behind her and closed the door, wanting to have this conversation in private. "Lying *is* a big deal, Emily. Proverbs tells us that the Lord hates lying lips."

Emily flushed. "It was just a little white lie."

"A white lie is told for selfless reasons," Charlotte explained, "to keep from hurting someone's feelings. Your lie to Hunter was told for a selfish reason, simply because you didn't feel like talking to him."

Anger flashed in Emily's gray-green eyes. "Well, I wouldn't have to lie to Hunter at all if he would just stop calling here so much."

"I think the reason he's calling is because you've led him to believe you like him as more than a friend."

Her flush deepened. "I can't help what he thinks. Ashley used to call me all the time too."

"You know that's different."

Emily turned away from her and shut her closet door. "I'm going riding with him later this week, so it's not like I'm purposely ignoring him."

"You need to make it clear to Hunter that you only like him as a friend. I know you feel Ashley hasn't been treating you very well, but that doesn't give you license to treat Hunter badly."

Emily didn't say anything. Her gaze focused on the floor in front of her.

Charlotte walked out of the bedroom, hoping she'd gotten her message across. Emily was playing a dangerous game, and Hunter wasn't the only one at risk of getting burned.

Chapter Sixteen

"I've got great news."

Wyatt sat on a bench near the playground with Christopher and Dylan on either side of him. A north wind made recess colder than usual, and they all huddled in their coats trying to keep warm.

Wyatt looked from one to the other, letting the suspense build.

"Well," Dylan finally said, "what is it?"

Wyatt grinned. "I got the copper pipes and wire we need to build our lightning rods. I helped my dad clean out his plumbing trailer last night, and he had a bunch of scraps left over from his job. I asked if I could have them to build stuff and he said yes."

"Cool!" Christopher exclaimed. He started swinging his legs back and forth to keep warm. "I'll print out the diagrams we found on the internet so we can get started building them."

"Do we need any special tools?" Dylan asked.

Christopher shook his head. "Just a hammer and some wire cutters. We've got those at the farm."

"Orrin has some too." Dylan said, referring to his stepfather. "He'll probably let me borrow them."

Christopher couldn't wait to get started on his new project. If the lightning rod worked, he planned to give it to Grandma and Grandpa so they could put it on the house or the barn.

"When can we start working on them?"

Wyatt shrugged. "I don't know. My mom probably won't let us do it at my house. She was kind of mad at my dad for giving me all those scraps and said it would just make a big mess."

"You guys can come over to my house tomorrow after school," Dylan suggested. "We can work on the lightning rods in my garage."

"Sounds good to me," Christopher replied. "I heard Grandpa say it was supposed to be warmer tomorrow too, so at least we won't be so cold. I'll ask my grandma if I can come over tomorrow and let you know."

"And I'll ask my mom," Wyatt said. "She'll probably just be happy to have me take all that junk away."

Christopher saw Trina Landrew skip by him and felt a twinge of irritation. Her fifth-grade class was currently in first place in the food drive contest, despite all the donations he'd gotten from church members. She'd obviously gotten some too, and that still didn't seem fair to him since he'd asked for them first.

"Does your mom want to give away more canned food?" Christopher asked Wyatt. "We need all the cans we can get if we want to win."

"That's because not everybody in our class brought ten cans like they were supposed to," Dylan complained, his legs moving too, but from his odd twitches rather than the cold.

Christopher nodded, certain that the additional three hundred cans would have put them way ahead of every other grade in the school.

His gaze moved across the playground, and then focused on the worst offender, Rachel Wells, who had only donated one can to the food drive so far. He'd made a secret chart of his own to record how much each student in his class had donated. So far, he was at the top of that chart, and Rachel was at the very bottom.

She stood against the brick wall of the school, only twenty feet away from them, trying to stay out of the wind. Another girl from their class, Liza Cummings, stood next to her dribbling a basketball against the pavement. Liza was on the bottom half of the list too, although she'd brought a lot more cans than Rachel.

All Christopher had to do was convince Rachel and Liza and a few other kids to bring ten more cans of food to class by Friday, and they'd win the field trip.

He really wanted to tour the television station and meet the meteorologist, but it didn't matter where they went as long as they got a day off from school.

Suddenly, Christopher realized that Liza and Rachel were staring back at him.

"Take a picture if you think we're so cute," Liza called out to him in her snottiest voice. "It will last longer."

Christopher averted his gaze, feeling both angry and embarrassed. Now Liza would probably think he liked one of them when he really just wanted to do his duty as class leader of the food drive.

After a moment, he got up and motioned to his friends. "Come on."

"Where are we going?" Dylan asked as both he and Wyatt scrambled to their feet.

"Just follow me," Christopher said, not wanting to approach the two girls without reinforcements.

He really didn't want to talk to them at all, but anything was better than letting them believe he had a crush on one of them.

Liza stopped dribbling the ball, cradling it in the crook of her arm as she watched the three boys approach. Rachel whispered something to her friend behind her hand, and they both giggled.

Despite the cold wind, Christopher could feel his cheeks burning. Dylan and Wyatt stood slightly behind him, and he could tell this was the last place either one of them wanted to be.

"Well?" Liza challenged. "Are you here to ask us to join your nerd club or what?"

Liza was the taller of the two girls and towered above Christopher by a good five inches. She loved playing basketball like her big brother and had the strength to prove it.

He turned to Rachel, who was shorter and seemed a lot safer to confront. "I noticed you've only brought one can for the food drive so far."

"So?" Rachel replied, staring him down.

He licked his dry lips. "So we need a lot more if we want to win. The class agreed that we were each going to bring ten more cans. You haven't brought any more since that first day."

Rachel tipped up her chin. "I never agreed to any such thing."

"Me neither," Liza said. "Besides, I've already brought, like, twenty cans."

"Nineteen," Christopher corrected her.

Liza turned to Rachel. "See, the kid really is a nerd. He's actually keeping track of how many cans each of us brings."

"Christopher is the . . . c-c-c-class . . . leader," Dylan stuttered, coming to his friend's defense. "He's supposed to count the cans."

Liza rolled her eyes and started tossing the basketball into the air. "C'mon, Rachel, let's go shoot some hoops. This is boring."

"Go ahead," Rachel said, pushing her bare hands into the pockets of her brown wool coat. "It's too cold for me to play."

Liza shrugged, and then deftly dribbled her way over to the basketball court.

Christopher breathed a sigh of relief after Liza left, feeling more confident now that it was three against one. He turned back to Rachel. "So can you bring ten cans tomorrow?"

"No."

"Just bring all the yucky foods from your house that you don't like," Christopher said. "That's what I've been telling everyone else to do."

Her eyes narrowed. "You're not going to tell me what to do, Christopher Slater. I don't care if you are the *class leader*. I already told you I'm not bringing any more cans."

Christopher could see it was a hopeless cause. No matter

what he said, Rachel obviously wasn't going to change her mind.

He glanced over at Dylan, still stinging from Liza calling them all nerds. "I guess some people are just too *selfish* to care about the hungry."

It was the wrong thing to say.

He knew it as soon as he saw Rachel draw her clenched fist out of her coat pocket. She punched him in the stomach.

Hard.

The blow made him fall to the ground, and for a long moment he couldn't breathe. He just lay there, his knees drawn up in pain.

Dylan grabbed his arm and tried to pull him up, but Christopher didn't want to move. He felt as if he was going to lose his lunch.

"Hey!" Wyatt shouted at Rachel as he backed away from her. "That wasn't very nice."

A loud whistle blew somewhere behind them, and the next thing Christopher knew the recess monitor was hauling both him and Rachel into the school.

"ARE YOU FEELING better yet, Christopher?"

"A little," he replied, although his stomach was still sore. At least he didn't feel like he was going to get sick anymore.

Mrs. Adkins, the school nurse, looked as if she didn't quite believe him. "Why don't you lie down and let me feel your stomach again?"

He did as she instructed, lying flat on the table as she

poked and prodded. It tickled more than hurt, and he bit down on his lip to keep from giggling.

"Any pain here?" she asked, pressing into his left side through his shirt.

"No."

She moved her hand to the other side of his abdomen. "How about here?"

Tenderness radiated from the spot, but he tried to be tough. "No, it's fine."

"Okay, you can sit up now." She wrote something down in a chart, and then reached out to pat his knee. "Don't worry. You're going to be all right."

If only that were true.

Class had started twenty minutes ago, but Christopher was too nauseated and too embarrassed by what had happened to go back yet. No doubt all of his classmates now knew what had happened out on the playground.

I've been beaten up by a girl.

Christopher hung his head, wishing he'd never been chosen class leader.

"Principal Harding wants to talk to you," Mrs. Adkins told him. "I'll be right outside the door in case you need me."

"Okay," Christopher said weakly.

A few moments later, Principal Harding walked into the nurse's office. He wore a dark blue suit with a white shirt and a red tie.

"Hello, Christopher."

"Hi." He shifted nervously on the table, not used to talking to the principal.

"How are you feeling?"

He shrugged. "I'm okay, I guess. My stomach hurts a little."

"That's what I heard."

The principal pulled a chair up next to the exam table and sat down. "I also heard that there was some kind of scuffle on the playground and that you were involved in it."

"I didn't start it," Christopher protested, hoping that Principal Harding wasn't going to call his grandparents.

"I know, but I'm trying to find out who did start it. The recess monitor couldn't see everything that happened, but she did see you fall to the ground."

She saw it along with everybody else, Christopher thought to himself.

"I've already talked to Rachel and Dylan and Wyatt," Principal Harding continued, "but they aren't saying anything. So I was hoping maybe you could tell me what happened out there."

Principal Harding was using his nice voice, not the voice he used when he told kids to stop running in the hallway. But it didn't matter how he sounded, because Christopher knew he couldn't squeal on one of his classmates.

Christopher looked down at the tile floor. "I don't really remember."

Principal Harding's eyes filled with concern. "You didn't hit your head, did you?"

"No," he replied. "We were just talking and then . . . I fell down."

"You fell? You weren't pushed?"

Christopher hesitated. "Like I said, I don't really remember."

Principal Harding stared at him for a long time, and then rose to his feet. "Well, if you do remember, will you come and see me?"

"Okay," Christopher replied, although they both knew that would never happen. If he tattled on Rachel, the whole class would hate him. Liza would probably beat him up, and she looked as if she could hit even harder than Rachel.

It just wasn't fair. He was only trying to do a good job as class leader. Now they'd lose the contest and everybody would blame him. Maybe Liza was right.

Maybe he really was a nerd.

Chapter Seventeen

On Wednesday afternoon, Emily hurried to her locker between classes to drop off her geometry book and grab her English book. She quickly dialed the combination on the lock and opened the door to make the switch.

"Hey, Emily."

Surprised at the sound of Ashley's voice, she turned around. "Oh. Hi."

Ashley hugged her books against her chest. "How are you?"

"Fine."

Emily hated the stilted conversation between them. They hadn't seen each other since that blowup at church. Emily had been avoiding Ashley ever since.

In truth, she felt a little embarrassed. She realized now that she'd overreacted when Ashley had asked her why she wasn't home on Saturday. All the loneliness and boredom and, if she was honest with herself, jealousy she'd endured because Ashley had a boyfriend had simply bubbled to the surface and erupted.

Now she wasn't sure how to make it right again without coming off as a complete loser.

"Look," Ashley began, taking a step closer to her, "the bell is going to ring soon so I just want to say . . . I'm sorry . . . for everything."

Emily had been searching for the right words to explain her behavior on Sunday, and Ashley had shown her how simple it really was.

"I'm sorry too," Emily said. "I didn't mean anything I said to you on Sunday. I was just . . . I'm not sure how to explain it."

Ashley flashed a relieved smile. "I'm not sure what happened to us. I know I've been spending all my time with Ryan, and I miss you. Can you come over to my house after school today?"

Emily didn't hesitate. "That would be great. Christopher is going to a friend's house after school, and then Sam is picking him up after he gets off work at the airport. He can pick me up then too."

"Great!" Ashley exclaimed as the bell rang. "That will give us plenty of time to catch up."

Emily couldn't wait to tell Ashley all about Pete and Dana's wedding plans and compare notes on the ridiculous outfit that Nicole Evans had worn to school today.

"See you after school," Ashley said, hurrying off to class.

Emily did the same, knowing she'd probably be tardy, but not caring at all. She finally had her friend back, and the world looked bright and sunny again.

"JUST PUT THE PACKAGES here on the porch," Charlotte told the UPS driver.

She watched him unload eight big boxes and wondered what in the world Pete had ordered. The combine had broken down again this afternoon, so Pete was in town picking up the part he needed while Bob drove the grain truck to the elevator to dump a load of corn.

"Please sign right here, ma'am," the driver said, holding out his electronic signature pad.

Charlotte signed her name and handed the pad back to him, wondering what Bob would say about all of this. "Here you go."

"Thank you," he said as he headed for his truck. "Have a nice evening."

"You too."

She stood on the porch, enjoying the southerly breeze. It was warmer today than it had been in a while, but she knew it wouldn't last long. Soon snow would blanket the ground. She just hoped it would hold off until after Thanksgiving.

She sighed, remembering Bill's phone call last night. He'd given her an update on Anna, who was doing fine, and he'd told her they probably wouldn't make it to the farm for Thanksgiving this year since Anna was supposed to stay in bed.

Charlotte understood, but she was still deeply disappointed. She'd been expecting to have the entire family around the table this year.

She saw Pete's pickup truck crest the hill and watched him drive toward the farm and turn into the driveway. He was just in time since she wanted him to put these boxes away before Bob saw them.

"Did you get the part?" Charlotte asked as he climbed out of his truck.

"I did."

She'd thought he'd just gone in to buy another belt, but the tarp tied over the bed of the truck concealed something much larger.

"What have you got under there?"

He grinned. "Wait until you see."

She walked closer to the truck while he untied the tarp and pulled it off. Her mouth dropped in surprise. "Kitchen cupboards?"

"That's right," he said. "I saw them in the window of the lumberyard when I drove through town. They were on clearance, so I couldn't resist."

"Oh, Pete," she breathed, wondering how he could afford them, even at clearance prices. They were a dark cherry color that would look wonderful with the gold walls, but Bob would blow a gasket when he saw them.

"Are you sure you can afford all of this? The UPS truck just dropped off some big boxes for you."

"Must be the tables and dinette set I ordered. I was hoping they would come today."

She noticed he'd avoided her question about the cost. He probably thought it wasn't any of her business, and he was right. Charlotte supported the fact that Pete was fixing up the apartment for Dana and really liked the changes he'd made so far. She still worried about the expense, but that was a worry she needed to keep to herself.

He pulled the tarp back over the cupboards and tied it

down. "I'm going to put the belt on the combine and head back out to the field."

"What about all this?" she said, pointing to the boxes on the porch and the cupboards in the truck.

"I'll unload it all tonight after I'm done harvesting." He looked around the yard. "Unless the kids want to do it."

"They're not here," she told him. "Christopher and Emily are visiting friends. Sam's going to bring them home after he gets off work."

Pete opened the passenger door of the truck. "Well, maybe they can help me carry this stuff up to my place later tonight. I'm ready to finish all the renovations."

"Are you sure you don't want to stay in the spare bedroom while you're working on the apartment?" Charlotte asked him. "It's going to be a mess at your place until you get it all done."

"I thought about it," Pete told her, "especially when I was painting. But you get used to the mess and the fumes after a while. I keep a fan in the window to keep the place ventilated."

"Well, you're always welcome if you change your mind."

"Thanks, Mom," he said, hopping back into his truck. He'd left the combine in the field rather than wasting time driving it back for such an easy repair job.

He took off, pulling out of the driveway before swerving a little to avoid the horse and rider on the other side of the gravel road. As the horse got closer, Charlotte recognized the rider as Hunter Norris.

He waved to her, and Charlotte walked to the road to meet him.

"Hello, Hunter."

"Hi, Mrs. Stevenson," he said, climbing down off his horse. He nudged the quarter horse off the road, and the horse bent down to start nibbling Charlotte's front lawn.

"It's a nice day for a ride."

"Really nice," he said, clearing his throat. "Is Emily here?"

"No, I'm sorry, she's not. She's at Ashley's house and won't be home for another hour or so."

"Oh."

The expression on his face told Charlotte that wasn't the answer he wanted to hear. He'd called Emily three times last night, and to her granddaughter's credit she'd finally quit making excuses and talked to him, although their conversations were short. Charlotte just didn't understand why Emily was playing with this boy's feelings.

"When I saw her at school this morning, she told me she'd be here."

"You're welcome to come over later this evening if you'd like," Charlotte replied.

"It will be too dark by then." A blush burned in his cheeks. "We were supposed to go riding together today right after school. I waited for her at my house and when she didn't show up I thought maybe she got held up here with her chores or something, but I guess that wasn't the reason."

He sounded so dejected that Charlotte wanted to give him a hug, but she sensed that would only make things worse and embarrass him to boot.

"Do you want me to give her a message?"

"No," Hunter said, climbing back up on his horse. "I think I got her message loud and clear."

"CAN YOU BELIEVE that outfit Nicole wore today?" Ashley said as the two girls grabbed some snacks from the kitchen, before disappearing into Ashley's bedroom.

"I know. It looked awful." Emily plopped herself down on Ashley's beanbag chair. "That girl has no fashion sense."

Ashley had been dating Ryan for only a few weeks, but it seemed like forever since they'd talked like this. Emily opened her soda and dipped her hand into the bag of sour-cream-and-onion potato chips that sat between them.

Ashley's brother, Brett, was helping Melody at the restaurant, so it was just the two girls alone in the house, giving them plenty of privacy.

"That science test was *so* hard today. How can anyone possibly remember the names of all those different kinds of rocks? I know I failed it."

"I'm sure you did fine. Besides, Mr. Campbell always has lots of extra-credit projects if you need to bring your grade up."

Ashley laughed as she grabbed another chip. "Ryan always calls him Mr. Chicken Soup. He even did it to his face once, but Mr. Campbell didn't think it was very funny."

Neither did Emily. She hadn't come over today to hear Ryan's jokes, no matter how hilarious Ashley thought they were.

"What colors do you think Dana should pick for her wedding?" she asked, ready to change the subject. "I've always liked the combination of pink and brown or turquoise and brown, but I really don't like brown tuxes—and what other color would the groomsmen wear?"

Ashley sat on the floor next to the beanbag, her back

leaning against the bed. "I'd want to pick a color that matched my groom's eyes. Ryan's eyes are brown, so I think the turquoise-and-brown combination would look really good."

Emily stared at her. "You've been dating him less than a month, so I doubt you have to worry about matching his eye color to your wedding colors."

Ashley blushed. "I was just using him as an example. I didn't say I was going to marry him."

"Good, because that would be ridiculous."

Ashley set down her soda. "Why would it? Do you think I'm not good enough for the Holt family?"

Emily rolled her eyes. "I never said that. If anything, Ryan's not good enough for you. He's the class clown."

"Everybody thinks he's really funny." Ashley rose to her feet. "Including me."

The mood had changed so quickly Emily felt as if she had whiplash. She felt frustrated that she'd come over to have girl time with Ashley and the subject had turned to Ryan Holt before she'd even been here five minutes.

"I think you're just jealous," Ashley said.

Emily stood up. "Jealous of Ryan? Now that is funny. He's probably only dating you to get help with English class. He never even noticed you before."

As soon as the words were out of her mouth, Emily wished she could take them back. "I didn't mean it," she said quickly.

But it was too late. Tears sprang into Ashley's eyes, and she bolted out of her bedroom and into the bathroom across the hall, slamming the door behind her.

Chapter Eighteen

"Wow, this stuff is cool!" Dylan exclaimed as Wyatt dumped out the lawn bag of copper tubes and wire onto the Lonetrees' garage floor.

Christopher reached into his back pocket to pull out the information about lightning rods that he'd printed off the computer in the school library that afternoon. The movement made him wince a little, his stomach still sore from Rachel's fist colliding with it.

The nurse had asked him if he wanted her to call his grandma, but he'd finally convinced her that he was fine and didn't feel any pain at all. It was bad enough that Rachel had made him fall down. He didn't want to add to his humiliation by having to be sent home from school.

He'd timed his return to class perfectly, leaving with a small group of students to go to the library. A few of the kids asked him what had happened, and he told them he'd tripped on something. Christopher wasn't sure they believed him, but as far as he was concerned it was his word against Rachel's. He was certain Wyatt and Dylan wouldn't say anything about it.

"Okay," he said, unfolding the paper. "It says here that lightning rods, which are also known as air terminals, should be put on the highest point of the building."

"Well, that's obvious," Wyatt said as he uncoiled a small roll of copper wire.

The wire was kinked in several places, evidence that it had been used before, but Christopher doubted that would matter for their project.

"Copper is the best conductor to use for a lightning rod," Christopher continued, skimming the paper for the parts that most interested him. "Especially for aluminum roofs."

"My roof isn't aluminum," Dylan said, picking up two skinny pipes and banging them together.

"Neither is mine," Wyatt added, picking up two copper pipes of his own to join the chorus of bone-tingling clangs.

Christopher had to practically shout to be heard over all the noise. "The lightning rod should be attached to the roof with a metal bracket and screws." He frowned, looking down at the jumble of copper scraps in front of him. "Did anybody bring brackets?"

Wyatt stopped clanging the pipes together. "I don't know." He knelt down on the floor and started sorting through the mess. Soon Dylan put down his pipes and joined him.

Christopher's ears still rang, but at least now he didn't have to shout anymore. "How about screws? Did anybody bring screws?"

"I don't see screws or brackets," Wyatt said, finally giving up the search. He rose from the floor, wiping the oily dirt off his jeans.

Dylan stumbled to his feet. "We don't need them until after we make the lightning rods anyway, do we?"

Christopher looked down at the diagram on his information sheet. "I guess not."

"Let's just get started," Wyatt said. "We can figure out all the rest later. I'm going to have to leave by five."

"Me too." Christopher stuck the paper back in his pocket. "My brother's picking me up."

Dylan bent down to pick up a pipe. "Let's get started then."

An hour later, Sam pulled into the Lonetrees' driveway and honked the horn of his sporty Datsun 240-Z.

"Sounds like your brother is ready to go," Dylan said, holding his shiny new lightning rod.

Christopher and Wyatt each had one too. Although none of them were complete, they'd accomplished enough to finish them on their own.

"Let's show him what we made," Wyatt suggested.

Sam was approaching the house when Christopher, Dylan and Wyatt emerged from the garage.

"There you are," Sam said to his brother. "Didn't you hear me honk?"

"Yeah, but we wanted to show you our lightning rods." He held his out for Sam to examine.

"Pretty cool," Sam said, taking it out of his hands. "But you guys know lightning rods don't really work, don't you?"

"Yes, they do," Christopher countered. "We read articles about it on the internet."

Sam laughed. "You should know by now not to believe everything you read on the internet."

"My uncle is buying some for his farm buildings," Wyatt said, "so he thinks they work."

"Well, maybe he's right," Sam admitted. "I'm just telling you what I heard. I really don't know that much about them. They do look a little dangerous, though. You'd better be careful."

To demonstrate his point, Sam playfully poked Christopher in the stomach with the tip of the long copper pipe.

"Ow!" Christopher shouted, backing away from his brother.

Sam rolled his eyes. "Oh, come on, Christopher. I hardly touched you."

That was true, but Sam had poked him in the exact same spot where Rachel had hit him with her bony hand.

Wyatt turned to him. "Maybe she broke one of your ribs."

Dylan nodded. "You should get an X-ray."

Sam looked from the boys to Christopher. "What are they talking about?"

"Nothing." Christopher took his lightning rod and headed for the car. "We'd better go. I still have to do my chores."

"So do I," Sam told him. "But we're not going anywhere yet." He turned back to Wyatt and Dylan. "Okay, spill it. Who is this *she* you're talking about, and what did she do to my brother?"

Wyatt and Dylan looked at each other and then at Christopher.

"I told you it's nothing," Christopher insisted, wishing Sam would just let it drop. He knew that the chances of that were slim. The only thing worse than the whole class knowing he got beat up by a girl was Sam finding out. Then he'd probably tell Emily, who would tell Grandma, who would tell Grandpa, who would tell Uncle Pete, who would tell Miss Simons . . .

Christopher shook his head, certain the whole town of Bedford would know about it soon.

Sam looked at him. "Either they need to tell me or you do. We're not leaving this driveway until I know what happened."

"Rachel Wells hit him," Wyatt blurted out. "Bam! Right in the stomach."

"He fell down like a rock," Dylan added. "It happened really fast, before me or Wyatt could do anything to stop her."

Christopher dropped his head, not wanting to see Sam's expression. He was probably embarrassed his brother was such a nerdy loser that he couldn't even stand up to a sixth grade girl.

"Then what happened?" Sam asked.

"The recess monitor took them both into the school," Dylan explained. "But nobody got in trouble because we all refused to talk and the monitor didn't really see how it all happened."

"I got hit by a girl once," Sam told them. "It was in third grade. She gave me a black eye."

Christopher looked up at his brother. "Really? I never heard that before."

Sam grinned. "It's not exactly something I went around bragging about. But I survived. A guy can't hit a girl back, so you probably did the smart thing in faking a fall so she didn't hit you again."

Christopher stared at Sam, taking a moment to understand that he'd just given him a cover for his playground duel with Rachel Wells. "Yeah, I hit the ground right away."

Dylan's brow crinkled in confusion. "It didn't look like a fake fall to me."

"Well, it's over now," Sam said. "Just try to stay out of her way from now on."

Sam didn't have to tell him that. Christopher had no intention of getting anywhere near Rachel Wells or her friend Liza. He just hoped *they* stayed away—far away—from *him*.

"It wasn't Christopher's fault that she hit him," Dylan explained. "He was just trying to get her to bring cans to school like everybody else."

"It doesn't matter anymore." Christopher started walking toward the car. "The food drive is over. Our class is going to lose. I'm done with it."

"Hold on," Sam told him. "The food drive doesn't end until Friday, does it?"

Christopher turned around to face him. "No, but there's no way we're going to win the field trip now. Our class is too far behind and hardly anybody is even bringing cans anymore."

"Is this field trip something you guys really want to do?"

When all three boys nodded emphatically, Sam said, "Well then, you can't give up yet. You still have two days to win this thing."

"I don't see how," Christopher muttered, his pride hurting a lot more than his stomach.

He didn't want to fail as leader and he didn't want to disappoint all his classmates either. Well, except for Rachel. And Liza. And Justin Taylor. He didn't care what they thought of him.

But deep down, Christopher knew that wasn't true. He wanted them to like him, or at least like him enough to stop picking on him. If he won the field trip for his class, they might not think he was such a nerd.

"Have you tried going door-to-door?" Sam asked them.

Christopher looked up at his brother. "What do you mean?"

"I mean start knocking on doors here in Bedford and ask people to donate food. You could start tomorrow right after school, before it gets dark." Sam jingled his keys in his pocket. "I'd hit all the businesses around here first, since they're usually willing to donate to a good cause. Lots of people sponsored the Diabetes Walk-a-Thon, remember?"

Christopher wondered why he hadn't considered going door-to-door before. He'd asked for cans from Miss Simons and from members of the church, but those were people he knew. He wasn't as comfortable approaching strangers.

"We could help you," Wyatt offered. "If the three of us go together it might be fun."

"I don't know," Christopher said uncertainly. The idea of going up to a stranger's door and asking for a food donation made him feel uncomfortable.

"Sounds to me like it's the only way left for your class to win the contest," Sam said, "but it's up to you."

Christopher looked at Dylan and Wyatt. "What do you guys think?"

One side of Dylan's body twitched as he pumped his fist in the air. "I think we should do it!"

"WE NEED TO TALK," Charlotte said, meeting Emily at the door. "Let's go to your room."

Charlotte saw Sam and Christopher watching them as Emily followed her up the stairs. No doubt they were wondering what this was all about. "You boys go ahead and start your chores," she told them. "We'll have supper in a little while."

"What's wrong, Grandma?" Emily asked, carrying a shopping bag from Fabrics and Fun in her hands. "Are you mad at me about something?"

"Not mad," Charlotte replied, closing the bedroom door once they were inside. "I'm just disappointed."

Innocent gray-green eyes looked up at her. "Why?"

Charlotte took a deep breath, hoping Emily hadn't stood up Hunter deliberately. "Hunter Norris was here earlier looking for you. He said you two were supposed to go horseback riding together after school."

Her eyes widened in horror. "Oh, no! I completely forgot. And we even talked about it at school today."

"That's what he said," Charlotte said. At least Emily's reaction seemed real. "He was pretty hurt, Emily, when he found out you were at Ashley's house."

"That was a big mistake," Emily admitted. "Ashley and I had a horrible fight. Even worse than the one at church last Sunday."

That was the last thing Charlotte had expected to hear.

The only silver lining in this incident with Hunter had been that it seemed Ashley and Emily were finally getting their friendship back on track.

"It can't have been that bad," Charlotte said, looking at the bag in her hand, "if you two went to Fabrics and Fun together."

"I went there after the fight," Emily explained, "when Ashley kicked me out of her house. Sam wasn't supposed to pick me up for another hour, so I needed something to do during that time."

Emily opened the bag and pulled out some colorful fabric. "I bought some material to make sofa pillows for Uncle Pete."

The print fabric was beautiful, with its color combination of sage green, cranberry, and gold. The pillows would be perfect accents for his newly painted living room. But Charlotte hadn't come up here to talk about pillows. "How did Sam know where to find you?"

Emily tossed the fabric and bag onto her bed. "I walked back to Ashley's house and stood on the corner of the block. She probably didn't even know I was there. Or care."

Charlotte saw tears well in Emily's eyes and reached out to give her a big hug. *Lord, why do the teenage years have to be so hard?*

"I'd better call Hunter," Emily said. "He might be the only friend I have left."

"I don't think that's true, but go ahead and call him. I'm sure he'll be happy to hear from you."

Charlotte headed downstairs to start supper, hoping Emily would be able to smooth things over with both Ashley and Hunter.

Emily followed her downstairs a few minutes later.

"Did you talk to Hunter?"

"No," Emily said in a tight voice. "His little brother answered the phone. When I asked to talk to Hunter he told me to hold on. Then he told me that Hunter couldn't talk to me because . . ."

Charlotte waited silently, watching the tears spill over onto Emily's cheeks.

"Because he was washing his hair."

Chapter Nineteen

On Thursday, Charlotte parked her blue Ford Focus along the curb in front of Bill's house in River Bend, grabbed the chicken casserole she'd made, and climbed out of the car.

She'd called this morning before she made the thirty-mile trip, not wanting to just show up at the door when Anna wasn't feeling well. Bill had answered the telephone, assuring her that today would be the perfect day for a visit and saying he'd leave the door unlocked for her. He had a meeting at his office at ten o'clock, so it made him feel better to know Charlotte would be there.

As she approached the house, she couldn't help but notice the lawn was perfectly manicured and looked as if it had been mowed recently. It seemed rather strange for November, but she knew Anna took great pride in her home.

She tapped twice on the front door, before cracking it open. "Anna? It's Charlotte."

"Come in, Charlotte," Anna called out to her. "I'm in the family room."

Charlotte walked to the kitchen first and placed the casserole in the refrigerator, marveling at how spotless the room looked. Even when confined to bed, Anna somehow managed to stay more on top of her housework than Charlotte did.

She made her way to the family room, where Anna lay in a hospital bed, the head of the mattress raised to a forty-five-degree angle.

"Hello, there," Charlotte greeted her. "How are you feeling?"

"Just fine," Anna told her. "Please have a seat. Do you need anything? A cup of coffee, or a diet soda? I can't get it for you, but feel free to help yourself."

Charlotte sat down on the sofa. "I'm fine, thank you. And you look wonderful. Much better than the last time I saw you."

Anna shook her head at the memory. "I told Bill that's the last time I travel to the middle of nowhere during this pregnancy." She shuddered. "I hate to think what might have happened if it had been anything serious."

"I'm just glad it wasn't," Charlotte said. She wanted to defend Bedford's medical services, especially since River Bend was hardly a metropolis, but she bit her tongue.

"I went straight to my obstetrician after I left the Bedford Medical Center," she continued, "just to make sure the baby wasn't in any danger. My OB told me I should go directly to bed and stay there until she gives me the green light to get up again." She laid her head back against the pillow. "So here I am."

"I'm glad your OB concurred with Dr. Carr."

"Bill has been so wonderful," Anna said with a happy sigh. "He rented this hospital bed and set it up in here so I can be with the family instead of exiled in my room. The girls have been quiet as church mice, trying not to disturb me. Of course, my mother's been keeping them at her house most of the time."

"That's nice of her," Charlotte said, happy to see Anna have so much energy, even if her words did tend to grate a bit. She was eight months pregnant, after all, and needed to be treated with patience. Then again, Anna had always been this way, so Charlotte couldn't really blame it on hormones.

"My folks have been a lot of help." Anna reached over to her bedside table and picked a purple grape out of the bowl. "Cooking meals and bringing over DVDs to keep me entertained."

"I'm sure you must get tired of lying in bed all the time."

"Very." She popped the grape into her mouth.

"I brought you a chicken casserole." Charlotte told her. "It's in the refrigerator. I wrote the instructions on a sticky note on top of the foil cover."

"That was sweet," Anna said, reaching for another grape. "Thank you."

Charlotte folded her hands on her lap, struggling to think of something else to say. She seldom spent time alone with Anna, their conversations usually buffered by the grandchildren or the presence of Bill and Bob.

Despite their differences, she truly did care for Anna and wanted them to have a good relationship. "I have an idea," she said at last.

Anna turned to look at her.

"Why don't the girls come to the farm for the weekend?

That would give both your parents and you a break, and we'd love to have them."

Anna slowly nodded her head. "That might work. We still have to pick up the baby furniture. Bill could bring Jennifer and Madison to your place and load up the furniture then."

"And Bob and I will drive the girls back to River Bend on Sunday afternoon."

"Great." Anna smiled. "Let's plan on it."

Something niggled at Charlotte, and then she remembered some plans they'd already made for Saturday. "Oh, dear."

"What is it?"

"I forgot that Bob and I are supposed to go to dinner with Dana's parents in Grand Island on Saturday. We've just gotten reacquainted with them, so I'd hate to cancel. Would you mind if the kids babysat the girls for a few hours?"

Anna grimaced. "I'm not sure I'm comfortable with that, Charlotte. You know how dangerous a farm can be." Charlotte opened her mouth, but Anna plowed ahead. "Emily or the boys could easily get distracted by a phone call or a computer game."

Charlotte bristled at the not-so-subtle criticism of her grandchildren as being irresponsible. Then she counted to ten and tried again. "I'll instruct the kids to keep the girls in the house the whole time. And Pete will be there for backup, just in case there are any problems."

"He will?" Anna mused. "Well . . ." She let her voice trail off. "If an adult will be there, I suppose we can let you have them for the weekend."

"Then it's settled," Charlotte said, forcing a smile. Despite her irritation, she did want to spend some time with her sweet granddaughters.

"Thank you for coming to see me, Charlotte," Anna said, smiling up at her, "and for the casserole. I really appreciate it."

She understood the signal to leave. Charlotte rose to her feet. "Have a good day, Anna, and please let me know if there's anything more we can do for you."

"I will," Anna promised.

Charlotte walked out of the house and then glanced at her watch. She'd spent more time on the road than she had visiting Anna. For a moment, she thought about stopping in at Bill's office to say hello, but decided against it. He probably had his hands full taking care of his pregnant wife and running the town and his law office. She'd see him on Saturday and have plenty of time to talk to him then.

"I'M NOT SURE this is such a good idea," Christopher said as he stood outside of the AA Tractor Supply store with Dylan and Wyatt. "They sell tractor parts, not food. They won't have any cans to give us."

The boys had walked downtown after school, ready to take their food drive door-to-door, only now Christopher was getting cold feet.

"But don't you know the guy that works here?" Dylan asked him.

"Yeah, his name is Brad," Christopher replied. "He's friends with my Uncle Pete."

"So this could be like a practice run," Wyatt said. "We'll try it out on him and see what happens. If he knows your uncle, then he probably won't yell at you or anything."

Wyatt had a point, Christopher decided. If nothing else, Brad might be able to give them some names of people who would be willing to donate some canned food. Only a few more cans had trickled into the classroom today, and they were still about sixty cans behind the leading fifth grade class.

That seemed like a really big number to overcome when he was standing there holding an empty sack.

"Let's either do it or go back to my place," Dylan said at last, "because standing around here is pretty boring."

Christopher agreed, squaring his shoulders before heading into the store.

Brad stood behind a long wooden counter, waiting on a couple of farmers. There was a peg board behind him with all kinds of belts and hoses and other machinery parts hanging from it.

The store smelled like diesel fuel and rubber tires, an odor that made Christopher wrinkle his nose. He'd been here before with his uncle and grandpa, and it always seemed to smell the same.

A group of farmers sat at a table in the far corner of the store, drinking coffee, eating peanuts, and talking politics. Christopher knew his grandpa liked to come here to visit with his friends, but he didn't see anything fun about the place.

"Hey there, sport," Brad said to him. "What can I do you for?"

Christopher walked up the counter and recited the sales

spiel he'd been rehearsing all day. "I'm Christopher Slater and our school is collecting cans for needy people."

He stared straight ahead at the strained buttons on Brad's red flannel shirt. "If you have some extra cans, could you please donate them to our class? Thank you."

Brad laughed. "Well now, that's quite a speech. You do know this is a tractor supply store, right?"

"We're just here to practice," Wyatt said.

"I see." Brad's eyes twinkled as he looked at the boys. "As a matter of fact I might have something to donate after all. Hang on a minute."

The boys waited while Brad disappeared into the backroom. A few minutes later, he came back with his arms full of peanut tins. "We buy these in bulk for our customers."

He placed two tins in Christopher's sack, two in Dylan's sack, and two in Wyatt's. "How's that?"

"Great!" Christopher exclaimed. At this rate, it wouldn't take them long to beat their goal of sixty cans. In fact, he should probably set the goal even higher just to make sure they came out on top.

"Good luck on your food drive," Brad said, "but pretty soon those sacks are going to get too heavy for you boys to drag around."

"We have a plan," Christopher said. "When they start getting too heavy, we're going to dump the cans we've collected at Dylan's house and then pick them up later."

"That sounds smart. Have fun," Brad said, turning away from them as another customer walked up to the counter.

The boys rushed out of the store, eager to take another look at their bounty.

"I can't believe we got six cans already," Wyatt said. "And we're just getting started."

"I know," Christopher said, more excited about going door-to-door now. Sam had been right: people did like to give to a good cause. This should be easy as pie.

Their next stop was at Mel's Place.

"Well, hey there, Christopher," Melody said, wiping her hands on the front of her apron as she walked over to greet them.

"Hi, Mrs. Mel," Christopher said.

"Are you boys here for a bite to eat?"

"No," Christopher replied. "I'm Christopher Slater and—oops, I guess you already know that." He cleared his throat and started again. "Our school is collecting cans of food for needy people, so if you have some extra cans, could you please donate to our class? Thank you."

Melody held back a smile. "You've come to the right place, boys. Come into the storeroom with me and I'll let you pick the cans you want."

Dylan gave him a high five as they followed Melody into the storeroom, where she had shelf after shelf of giant cans.

"I buy the industrial size," she told them. "You can take as many as you can carry."

To Christopher's disappointment, that turned out to be only two big cans for each of them. Now their sacks practically dragged on the ground.

"I think it's time to unload at my house," Dylan said, struggling with his heavy sack.

They slowly made their way to the Lonetree house. Christopher's arms were aching by the time they finally reached it and they dumped their haul in Dylan's tiny bedroom.

Brenda Lonetree stood in the door. "Are you done already?"

"No," Dylan told his mom, excitement making him twitch more than usual. "We're just getting started. We just got back from AA Tractor Supply and Mel's Place."

"Why don't you three split up?" she suggested. "You'll get a lot more cans that way and it will go a lot faster."

Christopher agreed and now felt confident enough to go out on his own. They left the house with their empty sacks in hand. Wyatt headed back downtown to solicit the other businesses while Dylan headed down one side of his street and Christopher took the other.

He hopped up the steps of the white mobile home that had three plastic pink flamingoes staked out in the front yard and knocked on the door, ready to recite his speech once again.

Only the words stuck in his throat when the door opened and he saw Rachel Wells standing on the other side.

Chapter Twenty

"What are you doing here?" Rachel hissed.

Christopher backed up a step, too shocked to form a coherent sentence. "I'm . . . uhmmm . . . I'm . . ."

"Rachel, who is it?" said a voice from behind her.

A woman appeared at the door who Christopher assumed was Rachel's mother since they shared the same eye color and curly brown hair.

"Just a boy in my class at school," Rachel replied.

Christopher wondered if Mrs. Wells knew that her daughter was punching people on the playground. He wasn't going to tell her, no matter how tempted he might be to get Rachel in trouble. Instead he decided to get his revenge on Rachel another way.

He smiled up at Mrs. Wells and took a deep breath. "I'm Christopher Slater and our school is collecting canned food for needy people. If you have some extra cans of food, could you please donate them to our class? Thank you very much."

Christopher took great delight in watching Rachel's face harden as he recited his plea for donations. She looked like she wanted to hit him again, but Mrs. Wells, instead of rushing off to empty her cupboards of canned food to give to Christopher, scowled down at her daughter instead.

"Did you tell him to come here?" she asked Rachel. "Because I already told you we're not donating any more of our food. You already got into trouble for taking that can of green beans."

"No," Rachel replied, her hands balling into tight fists. "I didn't tell him to come here. I don't even like him."

Christopher froze, not sure if he should just turn around and leave or wait until Mrs. Wells ordered him off her property. Mrs. Wells did not act happy to see him.

Then Rachel's mother looked up at him again, and her face softened. "I'm so sorry, Christopher, but it just doesn't make any sense for us to donate. We use the food pantry ourselves, so all our canned fruits and vegetables come from there."

"Oh."

The information took a moment for him to digest. He saw Rachel's cheeks turn a bright red before she ducked under her mother's arm and ran out of sight.

"Okay," he said, backing up another step and wishing he were a million miles away. "Thanks anyway."

He turned around and scampered down the stairs, his mind whirling. Now he knew the reason why Rachel had only donated one can of food, despite his badgering her for more. He remembered calling her selfish and felt sicker inside than when she'd punched him.

He was halfway down the block when Rachel caught up with him.

"Christopher, wait up," she commanded, gasping for breath.

He squeezed his eyes closed, anticipating another punch. Instead, Rachel Wells started pleading with him.

"You absolutely can't tell anybody at school about this," she said. "I'd just die if they knew. You have to promise me you won't say anything."

If Christopher wanted to, he could make her do anything right now. He could make her be his best friend, just to keep her secret. But Christopher wasn't that kind of person. Just the opposite, in fact. All he wanted was to make Rachel stop looking at him like that. He wanted to make Rachel feel better. "I won't tell anyone. I promise."

She didn't look convinced. "I mean no one at all. Not your friend Dylan or that goofy new kid Wyatt or our teacher or anyone."

"I promise," Christopher said again. "But you shouldn't be embarrassed about it. That's what the food pantry is for—to help people who need it."

"Yeah, like I want to be known as a charity case." She rolled her eyes. "We never had to go to the food pantry until my dad got injured at his job. Now he can't work anymore, and my mom has to stay home and take care of him. It just isn't fair."

Christopher didn't know what to say to her, even though he was all too familiar with how quickly life could change. One day you were in sunny San Diego with your mom, and the next you were on your way to Nebraska, a place you'd never been before, to live with people you hardly knew.

"I'm sorry," he said at last, unable to say it any better.

"Yeah, well, I don't need your pity." Rachel spun on her heel and walked back toward her house.

Christopher watched her go, realizing that he wasn't the only kid in sixth grade who worried about what other people thought.

CHARLOTTE WALKED UP THE STAIRS that evening to check on the kids and tell them good night. Bob was already asleep in bed, having put in another long day in the cornfield with Pete.

They were winding down with the harvest, and she'd reminded her husband that the two of them were making a trip to Grand Island on Saturday to meet Dana's parents for dinner whether the crop was all in or not.

She opened Sam's door first and found him stretched out on his bed, listening to his radio with his eyes closed.

"Good night, Grandma," he said without opening his eyes.

She smiled. "How did you know it was me?"

"I recognized your footsteps. Christopher can't go anywhere without sounding like a wild elephant, and I heard the sewing machine running in Emily's room, so I knew it couldn't be her."

Charlotte was impressed with his deductive reasoning skills. "You're pretty good. Maybe you should be a detective."

He arched a brow at the idea. "That might be fun. I could work for the police department or become a private detective and go into business for myself. I probably wouldn't even need to go to college for that kind of career."

"Well, keep your options open," she told him, closing the door again.

She moved to Emily's room, where her granddaughter had set up the sewing machine to make Pete's sofa pillows.

Now that Charlotte was busy hand-quilting the baby quilt, she wouldn't be using the sewing machine for a while.

"Look at this and tell me what you think." Emily tossed a square pillow at Charlotte as she walked through the door.

"Very nice," Charlotte said, admiring Emily's work. "I like the way you matched the stripes."

"That took some time," Emily admitted. "But it's not like I have anything else to do."

The house phone had been unusually silent these last couple of days with neither Ashley nor Hunter calling for Emily. Normally that phone rang off the hook, but Charlotte wasn't enjoying the silence since it made her granddaughter so unhappy.

"I'm sure it will all work out," Charlotte reassured her, tossing the pillow back to Emily. Then she noticed a bunch of photographs and graph paper on Emily's desk. "What's all this?"

"I've been working on some window-covering designs for Uncle Pete's apartment. I thought it would be fun to make them out of the same material as the pillows."

"They'll be lovely," Charlotte told her. "You're very talented, Emily."

"At least I'm good for something," she muttered, turning back to the sewing machine.

Charlotte walked over to kiss the top of her head. "You're good for a lot of things. Now don't stay up too late."

"I won't," Emily promised, lifting the presser foot on the machine.

A sigh escaped Charlotte as she left Emily's room. "Lord, what can I do for her?" she whispered. "Show me the way."

She found Christopher in his pajamas looking out his window when she walked into his bedroom.

"Anything interesting out there?" she asked, moving beside him. Stars twinkled in the night sky and she could see just a sliver of the moon.

"Not really." He looked up at her. "I don't think God is happy with me right now."

His words took her breath away. Christopher seldom talked to her about God. From the expression on his face, it seemed something was really troubling him.

"Let's sit down," she said, leading him to the bed.

Christopher sat beside her, his shoulders slumped. "I did a really bad thing, Grandma."

Charlotte braced herself, not sure what to expect. He'd been hanging around that new boy, Wyatt Carpenter, a lot. Maybe Wyatt was a bad influence. She didn't know his parents at all.

"What did you do?" she finally asked him.

He sucked in a deep breath. "There's this girl in my class named Rachel."

"Rachel Wells?"

He nodded. "Anyway, I was mean to her. I called her selfish and I got her into trouble with her mom and I think I made her cry."

Rachel's father had been seriously injured in an accident at a manufacturing plant in Harding six months ago. Apparently, the company had disputed his worker's compensation claim and it was dragging through the courts, leaving the Wells family without much income.

"How did all this happen?" Charlotte asked softly, aware that Christopher looked as if he were about to cry himself.

"It's because I wanted our class to win the food drive contest so we could go on a cool field trip. I was mad at Rachel because she wouldn't donate more than one can of food. That's when I called her selfish."

"I see."

"Then I went to her house today, although I didn't know it was her house, and her mom got mad at her because she thought Rachel told me to get canned food there. She said . . ."

His voice trailed off and he looked worried. "I'm sorry. I can't tell you what she said, Grandma, because I promised Rachel I wouldn't say anything to anybody. In fact, I promised her twice."

Charlotte nodded, fitting together the pieces of the story enough to figure it out on her own. "So that's why you think God isn't happy with you?"

He heaved a long sigh. "I think He's probably not happy with me because I cared more about winning the contest than helping people. We collected a lot of canned food today, but I don't think I would have ever gone door-to-door to ask people to donate if there wasn't a field trip for the winning class." He sighed again. "In fact, I know I wouldn't have."

As she listened to his stilted confession, Charlotte found herself praying again. *Lord, help me find the right words to comfort him. He's such a sweet boy. Help him find peace in his heart.*

"Grandma?" Christopher looked up at her. "Did you hear what I said?"

She circled her arm around his thin shoulders. "I did. Every word."

He lowered his head. "It's bad, isn't it?"

"People make mistakes, Christopher," she said gently. "You like to read about inventors, don't you?"

His head popped up, his eyes curious. "Yeah."

"Do inventors ever make mistakes?"

A smile quivered on the corners of his mouth. "Sure. All the time. That's how they figure out if something will work or not. Thomas Edison tried three thousand different ways to make a really good light bulb."

"Three thousand?" Charlotte echoed, impressed by Christopher's knowledge. "That means he must have made two thousand nine hundred and ninety-nine mistakes before he got it just right."

Christopher blinked as if that thought had never occurred to him before. "I guess so."

"That's because mistakes help us learn to do things better. I'm sure you'll think twice before you call someone selfish again."

He blanched at the very thought. "I'll never do it again."

"God knows we all make mistakes, Christopher," she told him. "Every single one of us."

He looked up at her. "Even Grandpa?"

"Even Grandpa." She smiled. "And the most wonderful part of all is that God will forgive us for all of our mistakes. He loves each one of us, even though we're not perfect. His love for us never ends."

His body relaxed at her words. "Really?"

The note of hope in his voice made her eyes sting with tears. Charlotte pulled him close and squeezed him tight, her love for him overflowing. "Really."

Chapter Twenty-One

Charlotte walked into Mel's Place on Friday morning, hoping to catch Melody Givens between the breakfast and lunch crowds.

"Hello, stranger," Melody greeted her as she walked out of the kitchen. "Long time no see."

"I know. Is this a good time for a visit?" She glanced at the older men seated at one of the tables playing cards. "I don't want to bother you if you're busy."

Melody waved away that concern. "Not busy at all. Those guys are all taken care of. Come on into the back room with me. Ginny can handle things for a few minutes."

The waitress was standing behind one of the card players watching the game unfold and advising him on which card to play.

Charlotte followed Melody into the back room, already feeling more cheerful. That might have had something to do with Melody's outfit. She wore a bright orange top and brown slacks, and two playful turkey earrings that dangled from her earlobes.

"Hard to believe Thanksgiving is next Thursday already," Charlotte said as they sat down at the small break table. "I haven't even planned the meal yet or done my shopping."

Melody grinned. "Russ is taking us out to eat in Harding for Thanksgiving this year. I told him this was one of my few vacation days and I didn't want to spend it in the kitchen."

"I don't blame you," Charlotte replied, wondering how to delicately broach the subject that had brought her here this morning.

Fortunately, Melody did it for her. "So what's happening with our girls? Emily never calls the house anymore and I haven't seen her for weeks."

Charlotte sighed. "That's what I wanted to talk to you about. I don't want to interfere in their friendship, but I'm afraid it may not last if something isn't done."

Melody stared at her. "Is it that serious? I just figured they had a little tiff."

"Has Ashley talked to you about it?"

Melody rolled her eyes. "All Ashley wants to talk about these days is Ryan Holt. I can't even have a conversation with her any more without his name coming up a dozen times. I don't think she's even aware of how much she does it."

Charlotte nodded. "I think that's part of the problem between Ashley and Emily."

"Ahhh," Melody said. "Now I understand. Ryan came into Ashley's life and my dear daughter started pushing Emily out of it."

"Not intentionally," Charlotte said. "And I think there's probably some jealousy involved on Emily's part. Ashley has a boyfriend now and Emily doesn't, so it only adds to the sting when Ashley doesn't have as much time for her."

"I need to talk to my daughter and explain the proper way to treat friends."

"Emily's certainly not blameless either," Charlotte said.

"She needs to learn that circumstances change when people begin new relationships. Ashley shouldn't have to choose between Ryan and Emily."

Melody leaned her forearms on the table. "Ashley also needs to get some balance in her life. It's almost as if she's obsessed with this boy." She shook her head. "We were hesitant to let her go out with him. Russ thinks she's too young to be dating anyone. Maybe he was right."

Charlotte knew there was no right or wrong in making these kinds of decisions. She'd started dating Bob when she was sixteen and that had turned out pretty well. But things had gone so differently with Denise.

"You can always second-guess yourself," Charlotte said wistfully. "We were so strict with Denise when she was a teenager. I often wonder if she would have eloped with Kevin Slater if we'd done less rule-making and more talking."

"Teenage girls are one of life's greatest mysteries," Melody proclaimed. "My biggest worry," she continued, "is that Ashley might like the Holts' lifestyle and wealth even more than she likes Ryan."

"How so?"

"Well, she's been over to their house several times, and she's always raving about their fine china and crystal and some great painting they bought at an art gallery that costs more than I make in a year."

"I'm sure those things interest her because she's experiencing them for the first time." Suddenly Charlotte realized what she'd just said and clapped a hand over her mouth. "Oh, I didn't mean it that way, Melody. You have a very nice house and . . ."

Melody started laughing again. "Oh, Charlotte, don't be silly. I'm not at all insulted. You're right. I don't have fancy china or crystal vases because those things aren't important to me. I just don't want them to take on too much importance for Ashley."

Charlotte certainly understood Melody's concern. It was so easy to get caught up in material things and hard to strike a balance. She thought about Pete and his endless purchases to fix up the apartment for Dana. How much was too much?

"So what can we do about these girls?" Melody asked her.

"I'm not sure there's much we can or should do, other than hope and pray they find a way to work it out."

Melody nodded. "Let's make sure we keep in touch, though, just so we know what's going on. Ashley doesn't tell me much unless I really push her."

"Neither does Emily." Charlotte sighed. "Although she did admit she said some nasty things to Ashley when she was at your house on Wednesday."

"Ashley didn't even tell me Emily had been there," Melody said, clearly exasperated. "Maybe it's time she and I do some of that talking you mentioned earlier. I think we need to get a few things straight."

"I didn't come here to get Ashley in trouble."

Melody's face relaxed into a smile. "Well, maybe I'm overreacting just a bit. I just hate it when my kids keep secrets from me."

"I think it would be hard to find a teenager who doesn't keep secrets."

She thought about Christopher, grateful that he still felt comfortable enough to share his feelings with her. His teen years weren't far off though, and she knew more challenges lay ahead.

"You're right," Melody agreed. "Let's plan to get together over Thanksgiving break. We can take Ashley and Emily with us to see a chick flick in Harding and then indulge in some girl talk at a coffeehouse afterward. That might be the perfect time for them to mend fences."

Charlotte liked the idea. "Give me a call next week and we'll set a date."

"Will do," Melody promised. Then she grinned. "And remember, Charlotte, it's not called interfering, it's called motherly love."

AT TWO O'CLOCK on Friday afternoon, the intercom crackled in the sixth-grade classroom, signaling that an announcement was about to be made.

Miss Luka put her book down, a smile playing on her face. "Listen up, everybody. I think we're about to hear the results of the food drive contest."

Christopher tensed, not sure if he was more nervous about winning or losing. He snuck a glance at Rachel Wells, who sat two rows over from him. She was chewing on the end of her pencil as she studied the math worksheet in front of her.

"Good afternoon, boys and girls," Principal Harding said over the intercom system.

There was an intercom speaker in every room, just above the white board at the front of the class. Miss Greinke, the school secretary, mostly used the intercom to remind students of an early dismissal the following day or to bring money to school if they wanted to buy something at the book fair.

Today, the announcement was really something special. "We have a winner for our first annual food drive contest," Principal Harding continued, "but first I want to congratulate all of you for the outstanding job you did in raising awareness about hunger in our community."

Christopher fidgeted in his seat, wishing he'd get to the good part. Adults always had to make things take longer than they should by using a lot of words when just one or two would do.

It was obvious he wasn't the only one who was impatient when Justin Taylor called out, "Just tell us who won."

"Justin," Miss Luka reprimanded him. "That's enough out of you."

"I know the director of the Adams County Food Pantry is very grateful for all the donations," Principal Harding said over the intercom, "especially with Thanksgiving just around the corner."

Christopher looked over at Dylan, who rolled his eyes at the long buildup to the announcement of the winning class. Miss Greinke had collected all the cans that had been brought in this morning so that Principal Harding could finish the final count in secret. He wanted the winner to be a surprise.

Christopher knew it was going to be close. He and Dylan and Wyatt had collected a lot of canned food yesterday going door-to-door, but he'd seen plenty of kids from other classes bring in more cans too—including Trina Landrew, who had borrowed a cart from Herko's Grocery Store to haul in all her cans.

"Now for the part you've all been waiting for," Principal Harding said. "By a difference of only two cans, the winner of the contest is . . ."

Christopher held his breath.

". . . the sixth-grade class!"

He just sat there as whoops and hollers sounded all around him. Several of his classmates clapped him on the back to congratulate him.

He snuck a look at Rachel to see her reaction, but she was still focused on her math worksheet.

"We did it!" Dylan said, leaning over to give Christopher a high five. Then they both did the same with Wyatt.

Miss Luka walked to the front of the class, all smiles. "I'm so proud of you!"

Principal Harding walked into the room. "Congratulations, sixth graders! Now where do you want to go on your field trip?"

Several students started talking at once. "The bowling alley!" "The television station!" "The mall!"

"Hold on." Principal Harding walked to the front of the classroom to stand by the teacher. "Let's do this in a more orderly fashion."

Christopher slowly raised his hand in the air, his heart beating a mile a minute.

"Yes, Christopher?" Miss Luka said. "Do you have a suggestion?"

He took a deep breath, hoping he didn't chicken out. "I think we should go to the city mission in Harding since the purpose of the food drive was to help them."

A few kids groaned around him, but Principal Harding held up his hands to silence them.

"Christopher was the sixth-grade class leader for the food drive," Miss Luka informed the principal. "I know he went to a lot of work to help the sixth graders win the contest."

That seemed to silence some of the groans as Christopher sat up straighter in his chair.

"Going to the city mission is an excellent idea," Principal Harding said. "I just read an article in the newspaper that the city mission is looking for volunteers, especially around the holidays."

Justin grimaced. "Can't we go to the bowling alley instead?"

"We'll take a vote," the teacher said. "That's the most democratic way. All those in favor of volunteering at the city mission for the class field trip, raise your hand."

Christopher raised his hand high in the air, along with Wyatt and Dylan and more than half of his classmates. He snuck another glance at Rachel and saw her slowly raise her hand.

The teacher did a quick count and then smiled at the result. "It's official! We're going to volunteer at the city mission."

Christopher couldn't believe that everyone had voted for his idea. He knew he'd always be the nerdy kid to Liza Cummings, and that Justin Taylor would keep bumping into him whenever he got the chance, but for the first time in his life Christopher felt like a leader.

Chapter Twenty-Two

"So what time do I have to babysit?" Emily asked as Charlotte washed the last of the Saturday lunch dishes.

"Bill and the girls should be here in another hour or so," Charlotte replied, rinsing a plate before setting it in the dish drainer. "He called a little while ago and said he had to catch up on some work in his law office and was running late."

Charlotte was running late too since she still hadn't dressed for their trip to Grand Island. Bob hadn't come in yet either. He'd told her during lunch that he just needed to run the grain truck into town and dump the corn at the elevator, then he'd be done working for the day.

That had been two hours ago.

She knew that during harvest the grain elevator could get busy, even on Saturdays. Bob had waited in line as long as three hours before, but she hoped there wasn't a line today because she didn't want to be late for the dinner with Chuck and Bonnie Simons.

"Do I have to make supper?"

Charlotte walked over to the refrigerator. "I already cooked up a big pot of beans and franks. The girls love that, so all you'll have to do is warm it up."

Emily wrinkled her nose at the dish. "What am I supposed to eat?"

Charlotte swallowed a sigh, tired of Emily's moping around today. She'd hoped babysitting Jennifer and Madison would help Emily take her mind off her problems. Instead, it seemed to be bringing her down even more. "I've got a bowl of egg salad, so you can make yourself a sandwich. There's also some banana pudding, if that sounds good to you."

"I guess."

Charlotte walked over to the table and picked up the list she'd made earlier. "I wrote down phone numbers: Bill's cell and house phones, Hannah's house phone, Dana's house phone and cell, and the Simonses' number, in case you need to reach us."

"What about Uncle Pete?" Emily asked, taking the list from her. "Will he still be in the field when you leave?"

"I'm not sure." Charlotte wiped some crumbs off the counter and shook the dishcloth over the sink. "I expect him to pull into the yard soon. He told me he only had a few acres left when I took his lunch out to him."

It made Charlotte feel a little guilty that he wasn't here yet since she'd told Anna he'd be around. Still, she knew Emily and the boys would keep a good eye on Jennifer and Madison. Pete was less than a mile away.

"I'm sure the girls will be fine," Emily said. "They're so good it's almost scary."

"Give them time. They'll be teenagers before you know it."

Emily rolled her eyes. "Very funny."

Charlotte glanced at the clock. She wanted to do a little shopping in Grand Island before they met Chuck and Bonnie for dinner, but if Bob didn't get here soon, there wouldn't be much time to do anything extra.

"Where are Sam and Christopher?" Charlotte asked.

"Sam just got back from his soccer game," Emily replied, "so he's in the shower. Christopher is outside playing somewhere."

"In this weather?" Charlotte asked. "I hope he wore a coat."

"He did. And a hat."

"Well, make sure those boys help you babysit when Jennifer and Madison are here. I told Anna that all three of you would help watch them. And they're to stay inside the house the whole time too."

"Yeah, I know." Emily looked down at her thumbnail, trying to peel off a patch of leftover nail polish. "I tried calling Hunter a little while ago to see if he wanted to come over and help me babysit."

"What did he say?"

"Nobody answered the phone."

Charlotte set out some snacks for the kids to eat later. "They must have gone out today."

"Unless they have Caller ID," Emily said, "and Hunter saw that it was me calling."

Charlotte looked over at her. "His heart got a little bruised, Emily. He just needs some time to heal."

Bob walked through the door and took off his seed cap. "It's getting chilly out there. The elevator manager told me there's snow in the forecast for tomorrow night."

"Ugh," Emily said with a groan. "I'm not ready for snow."

"It will come whether we're ready or not," Bob told her.

Charlotte glanced at the clock. "Speaking of ready, we both need to get that way. I'd like to leave in the next twenty minutes, if possible."

"You know it won't take me long to change," Bob said, heading down the hallway. "You're the one we're always waiting on."

Charlotte shook her head, wondering if Bob realized that he was only responsible for himself while she always had to make sure the kids had everything they needed as well as to get herself ready.

Just like today. All he had to do was come in from outside, get dressed, and go. She'd had to prepare meals, make a list for Emily, make sure the spare bedroom had clean sheets on the bed for Jennifer and Madison, and on and on and on . . .

She remembered her mother voicing some of the same frustrations. Charlotte knew that Bob had plenty of duties too, but the grass just always looked greener on the other side of the nuptial fence.

Twenty minutes later, Bob stood in the kitchen. "Charlotte, are you ready to go?"

"Coming," she replied, fastening the necklace Bob had given her for their last anniversary around her neck as she walked out of her bedroom. She stuck her head into the family room. "Bye, Sam. Have fun with the girls."

"Bye, Grandma."

"Charlotte, let's go," Bob prodded. "I've got the car warming up."

Her early irritation melted away at his thoughtfulness. There was nothing she disliked more than climbing into a cold vehicle. It always seemed to take forever for the heater to warm up.

She grabbed her coat out of the hall closet. "Emily, we're leaving now."

"Have a good time," Emily said as she descended the stairs.

Charlotte still didn't feel right about not being here when Bill and the girls arrived. She knew Madison and Jennifer would be perfectly safe with Emily and the boys until she and Bob got back from Grand Island, but it bothered her all the same.

"Do you want to take my cell phone with you?" Emily asked, obviously reading her mind. Or maybe she had just learned that her grandmother tended to worry a lot. "Then you can call and check up on us anytime you want."

"That would make me feel better."

"Charlotte!" Bob's voice was getting impatient. "The car's burning a lot of gas, and it's not even moving."

"I'm coming!"

Emily pulled the cell phone out of the front pocket of her jeans and handed it to her. "Here you go. I'm sure nobody will be calling me on it anyway."

"This too shall pass," she told Emily, quoting one of her late mother-in-law's favorite phrases as she dropped the phone into her purse. It always made her feel better to recite that bit of wisdom in times of trouble.

"There you are," Bob said as Charlotte walked into the kitchen. "Let's hit the road."

EMILY WAITED UNTIL her grandparents left, and then went in search of something to do. Saturdays could be so boring when you just sat at home.

"What's up?" she asked Sam as she reached the top of the stairs and saw him emerge from the bathroom. His hair was still wet and uncombed.

"I scored two goals today," Sam told her. "I was smokin' those defenders left and right. Too bad there weren't any college scouts there today."

"There are other things to do in college besides play soccer, you know."

"I guess," he said with a shrug. "I'm not even sure I should bother going if I can't play."

Emily wasn't in the mood to give a pep talk when she was feeling so down in the dumps herself. "I'm going to try to find Christopher. Do you want to come outside and help me look for him?"

"Nope," Sam said, following her downstairs. "I think I'll just surf the web for a while."

Emily took the time to put on a coat and hat before she ventured outside. The wind hit her as soon as stepped onto the porch, making her pull the hat farther down around her ears.

The blustery wind penetrated her coat, and she didn't plan to look for her little brother for too long before she went back inside the house. She was hoping he'd want to play a board game or something, anything, to make the time go a little faster.

She checked the barn first, thinking he might be keeping warm with the animals. As she opened the barn door, a puff of pungent steam escaped, warming her for a moment. The animals were in their stalls, but she didn't see Christopher anywhere.

When she walked back outside, Toby bounded up to her. "Hey there, girl. Where's Christopher?"

The dog started wagging her tail but just looked expectantly at Emily.

"I don't know where he is either," she said to the dog. Then she headed for the tractor shed. If nothing else, she could measure Uncle Pete's windows for the curtains and valances she was designing while she was there.

She opened the door to the tractor shed and walked inside, relieved to be out of the wind. The dog watched her for a moment, and then took off in the opposite direction.

"Suit yourself," she murmured, before closing the shed door. It wasn't nearly as cold inside the building, although it took a few moments for her eyes to adjust to the dimness.

Then she heard a sound, like two small stones scraping against one another.

"Christopher? Are you in here?"

"I'm over here."

Relieved that her search was over, she walked over to the corner of the shed, where she found him sitting on a bale of straw. A weird-looking copper tube lay at his feet, and he held two batteries in his hands.

"What in the world are you doing?"

"I want to see if my lightning rod conducts electricity. That way I'll know if it works or not. Sam doesn't think it will."

She pointed to the copper tube. "That's a lightning rod?"

"It sure is. I learned how to make it from a website on the internet. Dylan and Wyatt and I each made one. Lightning rods are for keeping lightning from hitting a building."

Now she was confused. "I thought lightning rods attract lightning."

"Oh, they do," Christopher said, as if he hadn't just contradicted himself. "See, you put a lightning rod on a house or building and the lightning will strike it and go off in a different direction so it doesn't hurt anything."

"How does it do that?"

He frowned at the question. "We haven't gotten to that part yet."

She smiled. "I see."

"Right now I'm trying to make electricity to see if the copper will get hot. That will mean it's working right."

"How exactly are you *making electricity*?"

"Like this." Christopher held the two batteries up, one in each hand, directly over his homemade lightning rod. Then he started hitting the ends together until a spark arced and landed on a piece of straw lying on the ground near the copper tube.

It immediately began to smoke, and Emily hurried over to stamp out the small flame with her foot. "Are you crazy? You didn't tell me it would start a fire."

"The spark was supposed to land on the tube." He frowned down at his lightning rod and shrugged his shoulders. "Okay, that was just a mistake I made as an inventor. Now I know that next time I want to create electricity

I need to do it outside and make sure there's no straw around."

The sound of a vehicle in the driveway saved Christopher from a lecture. Emily walked over to the dusty window and looked outside.

"Uncle Bill and the girls are here."

She headed for the door, motioning for Christopher to follow her. "Come on, let's go. I'm not leaving you alone in here to conduct any more experiments."

Chapter Twenty-Three

"I have a new coloring book," Jennifer announced when Sam opened the door to let them in.

He smiled at his young cousin. "Hey, that's pretty cool."

"You can color in it with me if you want," Jennifer told him, then she looked around the kitchen. "Where are Grandma and Grandpa?"

Bill set the girls' overnight bag on the floor. "I already told you, Jenn. Grandma and Grandpa had to go to Grand Island for a little while, but they'll be back soon."

Madison looked up at Sam. "So you're our babysitter? We've never had a boy babysitter before."

"I'm just one of your babysitters. Emily and Christopher will be babysitting you too."

Jennifer's eyes widened with delight. "We get to have three babysitters at the same time! That will be so much fun."

Bill walked over to the counter. "Looks like Mom put out some snacks. I was too busy to eat lunch today, so I'm starving."

"Help yourself," Sam told him as Emily and Christopher walked inside.

Jennifer immediately ran to Christopher's side. "Will you take me up to the toy box?"

"Sure," Christopher said, reaching for her hand. Then he looked over at Madison. "Do you want to come upstairs too?"

She nodded. "Yes, but I think I want Emily to take me."

Bill laughed. "Looks like these two are going to keep you hopping this weekend."

"That's okay, Uncle Bill," Emily said, taking Madison's hand as they headed out of the kitchen. "We can handle it."

Sam watched Bill open one of the storage containers that Grandma had left the snacks in. "I think there might be some egg salad in the refrigerator too."

"That sounds perfect," Bill said as he pulled a brownie out of the container. He grabbed a plate from the cupboard, appearing perfectly at home in the kitchen, and set his brownie on it.

Sam grabbed a brownie of his own. "I can help you load up that baby furniture when you're done eating."

"That would be great." Bill opened the refrigerator and started sorting through the contents. "Anna will kill me if I don't bring that baby stuff home and set it up tonight."

EMILY PULLED THE TOY BOX out of the closet in the spare bedroom and opened the lid. "It's all yours," she told the girls.

The toys were ancient, many of them the same ones that her mom and uncles had played with when they were little kids, but Jennifer and Madison didn't seem to mind. Emily had even seen Christopher in the spare bedroom a time or two playing with the one-armed GI Joe action figure and the faded Matchbox cars.

She looked over at her little brother, who was sprawled on the bed looking intently at the wrinkled sheet of paper in front of him. "What's that?"

"The plans for my lightning rod," he told her. "I'm reading what I should do next."

"I think what you should do next is throw that thing in the trash. It looks kind of dangerous to me, and you don't even know if it will work."

Christopher frowned up at her. "A good inventor never just gives up. I just need to tinker with it until it turns out right."

"Or until Grandpa catches you making sparks in the shed," Emily warned. "Then your tinkering days will be over because you'll have so many extra chores to do you won't have time for anything else."

"I already told you I'm going to do all my experiments with it outside."

"Well, good luck with that, because it's supposed to snow tomorrow, so you might just have to wait until spring."

She looked over at Madison, who was posing three vintage Barbie dolls on the windowsill as if they were fashion models.

Christopher tossed his paper aside. "Why are you so grouchy? Is it because Hunter isn't calling you all the time anymore?"

Her cheeks grew warm. "Don't be silly. I'm not grouchy about that."

As if on cue, the telephone rang, and Emily almost jumped out of her skin.

Christopher grinned. "Maybe that's him now."

Emily didn't move, refusing to get her hopes up again. Neither Ashley nor Hunter seemed to miss her as much as she missed them.

"I'll get it," Jennifer said when the phone rang a second time, hopping up from the floor where she had a row of Barbie dolls laid out.

Jennifer lifted the phone off the hook and said in a very polite voice, "Hello, this is the Stevenson residence."

"It's getting foggy outside," Madison said as she peered out the window. "Like a big, white cloud on the ground."

Christopher hopped off the bed. "I should check my weather station."

Emily looked over at Jennifer. "Who is it?"

Jennifer held out the phone. "It's for you, Emily. It's a boy."

Relief flowed through her that Hunter was finally talking to her again. She reached for the receiver. "Hello?"

"Is this the lady of the house?" said a strange male voice. "We're offering a very special deal on a fantastic new product called the Miracle Mop. It will make your floors sparkle and it can be yours for the low introductory price of . . ."

Emily hung up the phone, too disappointed to tell the salesman she wasn't interested.

"What's wrong, Emily?" Jennifer asked. "Didn't you want to talk to him?"

"No," Emily said with a sigh. "That's not the boy I wanted to talk to."

SAM SAT AT THE KITCHEN TABLE with a bag of potato chips open in front of him along with the container of brownies, which was now half empty.

"Want another soda?" Bill asked as he made himself another egg salad sandwich.

"Sure. I'll have a root beer this time."

Bill carried his sandwich and two cans of soda over to the table, setting a root beer in front of Sam before resuming his seat.

"Mom tells me you went on a tour of the University of Nebraska-Lincoln," Bill said, scooting his chair up closer to the table. "That's my alma mater, you know."

"Yeah, I knew you went to law school there. Did you like it?"

"Loved it." He picked up his sandwich. "I got my undergraduate degree there, too. UNL has a great business school."

That sparked Sam's interest. His inability to pin down a major was one of the reasons he wasn't sure about going to college. "So you majored in business? How did you know what you wanted to do?"

Bill held up one finger to signal that he needed to finish chewing before he could answer. A moment later, he swallowed, then said, "Actually, I started out as an agricultural business major on the east campus of UNL, thinking it would help me when I came back to Bedford to run Heather Creek Farm."

"You were planning to come back and take over the farm?" Sam gaped at him. "Like Uncle Pete is doing now?"

"Yeah," Bill replied, as if he could hardly believe it himself. "But after I'd been away from farm life a year or two, I discovered I really didn't miss it all that much, so I needed to rethink my career plans. One of my professors suggested I consider becoming a lawyer—and the rest is history."

Sam sat back in his chair, pondering Bill's words. He'd

been in college for two years before completely changing course, so maybe Sam didn't need to have his future career all mapped out before he went.

"What would you have done if that professor hadn't suggested you go to law school?" Sam asked. "Would you have stayed an agricultural business major or switched to something else?"

"I've wondered about that before. It's not like the professor sought me out and demanded that I consider law school. It was just a random comment when we were talking about something else entirely." Bill pulled a potato chip out of the bag. "I guess he liked my debating skills and thought I'd make a good attorney."

Sam knew that his Uncle Bill could prove pretty stubborn in a debate. He'd heard him and Pete go at it more than once when they disagreed about something.

"I suppose I would have picked finance or accounting, something in the business field. I liked those types of classes and I was pretty good at them."

"I don't really like any of my classes." Sam stretched his legs out under the kitchen table. "I'm just counting the days until graduation."

"Sounds like you have senioritis. That's pretty normal." Bill finished off the last bite of his first sandwich and reached for the second one. "Have you picked a college major yet?"

"Nope. That's part of the problem. There's no subject that really interests me. I think I'd die of boredom if I had to major in English or history or math. And I'm horrible at science, so that's out."

"What does interest you?"

Sam didn't hesitate. "Soccer. I love playing it, but I'm not nearly good enough to make it into a career as a professional soccer player, although that really would be my dream job."

"But you can use that love of soccer to help plan a career," Bill told him. "Just think about different types of jobs that might bring you into the world of professional soccer."

"Like what?"

Bill began to tick them off with his fingers. "Sports reporter. Athletic trainer. Sports agent. Coach. Publicist. Team promoter. Team manager."

"How about web designer?" Sam suggested. "Like creating and managing the website of professional athletes and teams?"

"There you go," Bill replied. "Look at how many soccer-related ideas we came up with in just a matter of minutes. It's all about brainstorming until you discover an answer that fits you and your skills."

Sam sat up in his chair, intrigued by all the possibilities. "Some of those jobs actually do sound pretty cool."

"The great thing about college is that you start out with core classes that everyone takes, along with classes in fields that interest you. That gives you the flexibility to change your major without having to start from square one."

Sam hadn't thought about it that way. The guidance counselor at school always put so much emphasis on the importance of choosing the right major, but Sam liked Bill's approach to college better.

"And I wouldn't give up on playing soccer in college, either."

"What do you mean?"

"Some colleges have a walk-on program that allows students to practice with the team and try out for a spot even if they weren't initially recruited for one. I know UNL uses the walk-on program for football and the Huskers have gotten a lot of premier players that way."

"I guess it wouldn't hurt to give it a shot if the college I choose has a walk-on program."

"Or you could play recreational soccer. UNL has a great intramural program for students with just about every sport you could imagine."

"Yeah, they showed us the indoor field at the student recreation center during our tour. It was pretty cool."

He could tell that Bill was really pushing him to go to UNL, but he appreciated all the advice. It was nice to talk to someone who had actually experienced college life there, even it if was before Sam was born.

"Just keep all your options open," Bill told him, pushing his empty plate away. "You'll get it all figured out."

Sam hoped he was right. At this point, he was glad he still had a few more months to think about it.

"I suppose I'd better load up the car and head back to River Bend," Bill said, rising to his feet. "Anna will be wondering what's taking me so long.

Bill carried his plate over to the kitchen sink and rinsed off the bread crumbs and pickle juice. Then he looked out the kitchen window. "What is *that*?"

The odd tone of Bill's voice made Sam jump up from the table. "What's wrong?"

Chapter Twenty-Four

Sam looked out the window in horror at the grayish-white cloud of smoke billowing up from the tractor shed. He couldn't see any flames, but there was no doubt what was going on.

"Where are the girls?" Bill cried, looking frantically around the kitchen. "Are they out there?"

Sam had never seen his uncle so panicked. "They're upstairs with Emily and Christopher," he reminded him, racing to the phone. He picked up the receiver and tossed it to Bill.

"You call 911," Sam told him, already headed down the hallway. "I'll drive out to the field to get Uncle Pete."

Sam took the stairs two at a time, adrenaline rushing through his body. He didn't know how the fire had started, but the way the wind was blowing today meant it could spread very easily.

Emily met him at the landing. "What's going on? I heard Uncle Bill shouting a minute ago."

"The tractor shed is on fire."

"On fire!" Her eyes widened in shock. "Oh my gosh! Madison told us there was a cloud on the ground, but I just thought a fog was rolling in. Then the phone rang, and I forgot all about it."

Sam didn't have time to stand there and listen. He edged around his shocked sister and raced to his bedroom to retrieve his car keys.

He couldn't find them.

Clothes littered the floor and his desk was a chaotic mess of books and papers. He swept his desk clear, but his keys weren't there. They weren't on his dresser either, or inside his backpack.

Emily stood in the doorway watching him, her face pale. "What should we do?"

Sam muttered under his breath, remembering all the times his grandma had bugged him about keeping his room clean. He stood there for a moment, trying to allay his anxiety long enough to remember where he'd put his car keys.

Think, Sam, think!

His adrenaline subsided long enough for the obvious solution to come to him. "I'll drive Uncle Bill's car to the field to get Uncle Pete. He's calling 911, so the fire department should be here soon."

Why didn't he hear sirens yet?

But he knew the answer. Only a minute or two had passed since Bill saw the smoke, and it took time for the volunteer firemen to get to the station once they received the call.

He heard the sound of a loud engine and looked out his bedroom window to see the combine about a half mile down the road. Relief washed over him that Pete was on his way home. Pete was a volunteer fireman. He'd know what to do.

Sam hurried over to the spare bedroom and motioned for Emily and Christopher to come over to him.

"You guys stay up here," he said in a low voice, not wanting to scare Jennifer and Madison, who were playing with the Barbie dolls.

Christopher's wide eyes told Sam that Emily had let him know about the fire. He looked so scared that Sam hurried to reassure him.

"Don't worry," he said. "The fire department is on its way, and Uncle Pete and Uncle Bill are both here." Then he turned to Emily. "Keep a close watch out the window. If there's any sign that the fire is spreading, then you and Christopher need to take the girls outside and stand in the field across the road until help comes."

"Where will you be?" Christopher asked.

"I'll be waiting in the yard for the fire department," Sam told him, "in case they need any help. Now promise me you guys will go outside if there's any sign of the fire spreading toward the house."

Emily nodded, her expression grim but resolute. "We will, Sam. You don't have to worry about us or the girls. I'll make sure they're all right."

"Me too," Christopher squeaked. "Now promise us you'll be careful."

Sam reached out to ruffle his hair. "I promise."

WHEN SAM REACHED the driveway, he found Uncle Bill watching the smoking building, his hands on his hips and indecision etched on his face.

"I don't know what to do!" Bill cried helplessly. "I was

going to get the hose, but if it's an oil fire, water would just make it worse."

"Did you call 911?" Sam asked him.

Bill nodded. "The dispatcher said the fire department would be on their way soon, but at this rate, the building might be gone before they get here."

"There's Uncle Pete," Sam said as the combine turned into the driveway. It came to an abrupt stop.

Pete jumped out of the cab, bypassing the ladder and almost falling as he made the four-foot leap to the ground. Then he ran up to Sam and Bill.

"What's going on?" Pete shouted. "What happened?"

"We don't know," Sam told him. "We just saw the smoke and called the fire department."

Without another word, Pete ran toward the building.

Bill took a step forward. "What are you doing, you idiot? Trying to get yourself killed?"

But Pete didn't answer him. Instead, he pulled his coat sleeve down around his left hand and used that covered hand to slide the door of the tractor shed open. Then he stood back to assess the situation inside the building.

"He's being careful," Sam told Bill, his heart pounding in his chest. "He knows what he's doing. He covered his hand in case the metal door handle was hot."

Sirens sounded in the distance and relief flooded through Sam. "It's the fire department. They should be here soon." Then, to his amazement, Sam saw Pete pull his handkerchief from his pocket, tie it around his mouth and nose, and rush into the shed.

"Pete, get back here!" Bill shouted to his brother as both he and Sam moved nearer to the open doorway of the shed.

Sam could feel the heat from the fire on his face and the acrid smoke invaded his nostrils, making him cough and choke. Then he heard the sound of the tractor starting up, and a moment later, Pete drove the big machine out of the shed.

"He's saving the tractor," Bill said incredulously, watching as Pete drove it a safe distance away and climbed down out of the cab.

The heat from the fire caused the windows in Pete's apartment to shatter, the shards of glass falling to the ground below.

The sound of the sirens grew louder as Pete lifted the handle of the water hydrant near the barn. The long hose that was used to fill the water trough for the livestock was already attached.

Pete picked up the end of the hose, spraying himself down from head to foot despite the cold, then he headed back into the shed.

Sam could see him hosing down the walls and the ceiling, trying to douse every spot of the building with water.

"He's not trying to put out the fire, he's trying to slow down the flames," Bill said. "Why didn't I think of that?"

Two fire trucks finally arrived on the scene, the crews going into action. They unrolled the fire hose and approached the building.

As soon as Pete saw them, he ran out of the building. "Go! Go! Go!" he shouted to them. "Watch out for the glass."

The firemen hurried toward the window with the fire hoses, the high-pressure streams already hitting the building.

Sam watched Pete get out of the way and drop down on his knees in exhaustion. He and Bill hurried over to him.

"Are you all right?" Bill asked, placing one hand on his brother's shoulder to steady him. "Do you need to go to the medical center?"

"No," Pete rasped, his voice raw. Ash from the fire smeared his face and hands. "I'm . . . all right."

"You were awesome, Uncle Pete!" Sam exclaimed. "You saved the tractor."

Pete closed his eyes. "And lost everything else."

BOB AND CHARLOTTE drove down Heather Creek Road. She froze as they passed two fire trucks coming toward them, away from the farm.

"Maybe it wasn't that bad," Charlotte breathed, her whole body tense with worry.

Emily had called them on their way to Grand Island, using the number for the cell phone she'd given Charlotte. She'd assured Charlotte that everyone was safe, and then she burst into tears.

As soon as Charlotte relayed the message to Bob, he'd made a U-turn on the highway and raced back to Heather Creek Farm. Charlotte had prayed the whole way, wondering what they'd find when they got there.

As they crested the hill, Bob pointed ahead when the farm came in to view. "Look at that," he exclaimed. The tractor shed still stood upright, but it was a black, hollowed-out shell.

"Oh, Bob!" Charlotte cried, her heart aching at the sight of the building that had been on the farm for as long as she could remember. "Look."

"I see it," he said tightly, his fingers squeezing the steering wheel until his knuckles were white.

Neither one of them spoke another word until they reached the farm. When Charlotte climbed out of the car, she couldn't help staring at the tractor shed, trying to make sense of it. The doors were open, what was left of the doors anyway, but inside was just a black void.

Bob was staring too. Then he said, "The tractor's not there."

"Did it burn up?"

"No," he replied. "We'd see the wreckage if it had burned." Then he took a look around the yard. "There it is, safe and sound."

Charlotte followed his gaze and saw the tractor looking just like she'd remembered, without a mark on it.

Christopher emerged from the house, running over to Charlotte and throwing his arms around her waist. "I've been so scared. I didn't know what to do."

She cradled her arms around him. "It's all right now."

"Where is everybody?" Bob asked him.

Christopher turned around to face his grandpa, his back still pressed against Charlotte. "They're inside the house cleaning up. The fire department just left."

"We saw them." Bob started walking toward the house. "Let's go inside where it's warm."

"Wait," Christopher called after him, still glued to Charlotte's side. "I have to tell you something."

She could feel his body shaking and wondered if the fire had sent him into some kind of shock. As Bob turned around, Charlotte knelt down beside Christopher so she was at eye level with him.

"What is it?" she asked softly. "What do you want to tell us?"

"I did it," he confessed, tears streaming down his cheeks. "I started the fire."

Chapter Twenty-Five

"Pete's a hero," Bill announced, seated beside his brother at the kitchen table. "I wouldn't have believed it if I hadn't seen it with my own eyes."

"Thanks," Pete said wryly.

Charlotte refilled Bob's coffee cup, her gaze falling on Pete. He'd taken a shower and changed into a pair of Bob's pants and a shirt, but he still looked worn out and shell-shocked. Little wonder, since his apartment had just literally gone up in smoke.

Bob's clothes were too big for him, but Pete didn't have anything else to wear besides the work clothes Charlotte had thrown into the washing machine. They'd stunk of smoke, and she planned to put them through at least two wash cycles to try and get the odor and ash out of the fabric.

Sam and Emily sat at the table with the adults but sipped hot cocoa instead of coffee. Charlotte had set a plate of brownies on the table too, but nobody seemed to have much of an appetite.

Thank you, Lord, for keeping them all safe.

She'd been on the edge of tears since they'd arrived back at the farm, especially when Christopher had clung to her while spilling out his story.

When she'd finally calmed Christopher down, she'd sent him into the family room to watch a Disney movie with Jennifer and Madison, who seemed oblivious to all the drama. The girls were laughing at the movie and, to her relief, she'd even heard Christopher giggling a time or two.

She knew it was just a temporary escape from reality for him. Only Charlotte and Bob knew about his claim that he'd started the fire. Soon they'd have to share it with the rest of the family.

As she stood near the doorway, she could hear one of the animated characters in the movie crooning, "Just keep swimming. Just keep swimming . . ."

It was good advice about moving forward no matter how many obstacles got in your way. The loss of the tractor shed and Pete's apartment seemed like one of the bigger obstacles they'd faced in a while.

"Just keep praying," Charlotte murmured to herself, knowing that was good advice too.

"You should have seen him," Bill continued, his voice filled with awe. "Pete raced right into that burning building and drove the tractor to safety without getting a scratch on it."

Charlotte shuddered at the risk her son had taken for a piece of machinery, no matter how expensive. The ceiling could have fallen in on him, or he could have been overcome by smoke inhalation.

"Then he grabbed the hose," Bill said, "and I thought he was nuts because there was no way he was going to put out that fire with that little hose. But instead, he started wetting down the walls and ceiling to slow down the fire. The fire chief told us that action probably stopped the fire from spreading to other buildings on the farm."

Sam looked over at Pete. "I can't believe you remembered all that stuff."

Pete shrugged. "It was all my training with the volunteer fire department. I didn't even think about it. I just did it."

"It never even occurred to me to get the tractor out of there," Bill said ruefully. "It's been so long since I drove one, I'm not sure I remember how to start it."

"I could have done it," Sam said. "I *should* have done it when we first saw the smoke."

"No," Charlotte said firmly, unable to hold her tongue anymore. "That's a very dangerous and very foolish thing to do."

Her voice was shaking, but she couldn't help herself. She'd already lost one child, she couldn't handle losing another.

"I'm okay, Mom," Pete said dully. "The tractor didn't have insurance on it, so I had no choice but to get it out of there."

"What?" Bill gaped at him. "The tractor is uninsured?" His knuckles turned white around his coffee cup. "It must be worth more than some houses cost in River Bend."

"Forty thousand dollars," Pete said, his voice flat. "But none of the machinery is insured. You have to make tough decisions so the balance sheet looks good for the bank. We had to find a way to cut expenses."

"Insurance premiums can eat you alive on a farm," Bob said, adding his two cents' worth to the conversation. "Fire and flood, life insurance, crop insurance, not to mention health insurance, which is almost unaffordable for a family farmer."

Bill rubbed a hand over his face. "Still, you can't afford to lose everything either. What if that tractor had burned up in the fire? Would you have the money to buy another one?"

"No," Pete said. "That's why I ran into a burning building to get it."

Charlotte wished Dana were here to comfort him. She'd gone to Lincoln for the weekend to visit her cousin and attend a bridal show. Both she and Pete had tried calling Dana, but no one had been able to reach her yet. Bonnie Simons had promised to keep trying when Charlotte phoned her to tell them the reason they hadn't made it to Grand Island.

"But the tractor shed was insured, right?" Bill looked between his father and brother.

"Yes," Bob replied, "but only for the minimum amount."

"It won't be enough to cover the loss of my apartment," Pete said bitterly. "The fire chief told me it was a total loss. My clothes. My furniture. All the renovation materials I bought to make the place nice for Dana." He swallowed hard. "All gone."

Charlotte's heart went out to him, knowing how hard he'd worked to make the place ready for his new bride, not to mention all the money he'd spent.

Bill seemed completely perplexed. "You take a real gamble if you don't insure your residence."

Bob snorted. "No insurance company was going to pay out much for a fifty-year-old apartment above a tractor shed. It wasn't worth fifty dollars until Pete started pouring money into it. Now that's gone too."

A muscle twitched in Pete's jaw. "I get it, Dad. You think

I spent too much money. Well, I guess you've proven your point. I used a lot of my savings to fix up my apartment, and now I have nothing to show for it."

"I'm still working on your sofa pillows," Emily said, trying to cheer him up.

"I appreciate that, Emily," Pete said. "I just wish I had somewhere to put them."

Charlotte was ready to keep moving forward. It wouldn't do Pete any good to keep dwelling on what he had lost. "You can stay in the spare bedroom until you figure out what to do next. Your dad and I will be happy to have you."

"Thanks," Pete told her. "That reminds me. The fire marshal will be out here tomorrow to investigate. Until then, no one is allowed to go anywhere near the tractor shed."

"Not even you?" Sam asked.

"Not even me." Pete sighed. "They don't want people tramping in and out of there because it might compromise the evidence."

Emily slid down in her chair. "What kind of evidence do you mean?"

Pete shrugged. "Evidence of what started the fire. That's what the fire marshal will be coming here to find out. Then he'll make his report and we'll all know exactly what happened."

Bob leaned forward, resting his arms on the table. "I think we may already know what happened," he said in a low voice. "Christopher told us when we were outside."

Pete turned to look at him. "Told you what?"

"It was an accident," Emily blurted. "We didn't mean to set the tractor shed on fire."

Charlotte turned in surprise to her granddaughter. "You were there too?"

Emily blinked. "Yeah, didn't Christopher tell you that?"

"No," Bob intoned. "He left that part out of his story." Then he leaned toward the hallway. "Christopher, will you come in here, please?"

They all waited in silence until Christopher appeared in the doorway. He didn't come any farther, a stark expression of fear on his face. "Yes?"

"It seems we didn't get the whole story from you about what happened in the tractor shed."

Christopher's gaze flicked to his sister and then down to the floor.

"Well?" Bob prodded. "Are you ready to tell us everything?"

"Yes," he replied, in the voice of someone destined for the gallows.

Charlotte patted the chair next to her. "Come sit by me, Christopher. I'll pour you some hot cocoa."

He didn't look at anyone at the table as he made his way to the chair and sat down.

"I didn't mean to do it," he said, talking to the floor. "I was trying to make electricity to see if my lightning rod would work."

Bill looked confused. "How were you making electricity?"

"He wasn't doing anything dangerous on purpose," Emily interjected before Christopher had a chance to explain. "He was hitting two batteries together to create a spark. The spark was supposed to land on the copper tube." She waved a hand in frustration. "It's really hard for me to explain."

"I think we get the gist," Sam told her.

Bob looked at Emily. "So what were you doing in there?"

"Emily didn't do anything," Christopher said, coming to the defense of his sister. "She told me it was dangerous and that I had to stop."

"But only after I saw one of the sparks ignite a piece of straw," Emily confessed. "I stomped on it with my shoe really good and thought I put the flame out... but I guess I didn't."

Pete pushed his half-full coffee cup away. "And here I thought all that paint and varnish I've been using in my apartment ignited some rags and caused the fire."

"Maybe we'd better wait and see what the fire marshal says before we jump to any conclusions," Bob said.

"That's probably a good idea," Bill agreed. "Then we'll have a better idea what happened."

Bob turned to Christopher. "I want you to throw that silly lightning rod away," he said sternly. "Do you hear me? It's not something a boy should be playing around with."

Christopher hung his head. "I can't, because it's still in the tractor shed and Uncle Pete told us nobody could go in there."

"Then we'll have to wait until after the fire marshal completes his investigation."

Charlotte set a cup of hot cocoa in front of Christopher and slid into the chair next to him, her arm resting across his shoulders. "Thank God no one was hurt. That's what's really important in all of this. Buildings and clothes and furniture can all be replaced, but no one can replace family."

"Amen," Bill said. Then he rose to his feet. "On that note, the girls and I had better get going."

"They aren't staying over?" Charlotte asked.

"I think I'd like to keep the girls close to home tonight after all." He lowered his eyes to the table. "I hope you understand."

"I do," Charlotte said quietly. "We'll look forward to having them stay with us soon."

After Bill left, Pete went outside to clean the stalks out of the combine and winterize it. Bob offered to help him, but Pete told him to stay inside and keep warm. Charlotte told him supper would be ready soon, but he declined that too. She sensed that her son wanted to be alone to mourn the loss of his home in private.

After a supper of franks and beans, the rest of the family drifted out of the kitchen.

Bob went off to take a nap in the recliner while Christopher, Sam, and Emily decided to go up to their bedrooms. Charlotte found that a little strange for so early on a Saturday, but she knew it had been a traumatic day for all of them.

She watched them climb the stairs together, sensing that the older two had closed ranks to protect Christopher, which was only natural. She hated to feel that there were any divisions between them. They'd come such a long way since she and Bob had brought them to Heather Creek Farm.

Now she wondered how much further they had to go.

Chapter Twenty-Six

When Sunday afternoon arrived, members of the Bedford Community Church, along with many friends and neighbors, came to Heather Creek Farm bearing gifts.

It was one of the rare Sundays that Charlotte and Bob hadn't attended worship service, still feeling the grandkids were too rattled by the fire to be around a lot of people.

Instead, people came to them, and Charlotte was surprised to feel grateful for the company. Bob sat out on the porch visiting with people who stopped by while Charlotte worked in the kitchen with Hannah.

"Look at all this food," Hannah said, putting another casserole dish into the freezer. "Why, you won't even have to cook Thanksgiving dinner this year. Your freezer runneth over."

Charlotte laughed, feeling better than she had yesterday. Although Christopher's part in starting the fire still weighed on all of them, the family was starting to bounce back from the shock of what had happened.

She cut up a pan of butterscotch bars to take upstairs to the kids. Sam and Emily had stayed by Christopher's side all day, playing games with him and trying to keep his spirits up.

Pete was still down in the dumps, but Dana was back from Lincoln and had taken him with her to Grandma Maxie's house for lunch. Charlotte hoped that getting away from the sight of his charred home for a little while would help cheer him up.

"Everyone has been so generous," Charlotte said, trying to make room on the counter for another frosted cake. "They've given us food and clothing and even furniture for Pete when he figures out where he's going to live."

"That's God working—through the people in this community and right here in this house," Hannah told her.

Charlotte nodded, knowing it was true. "I'm just so grateful."

"I'm just relieved there wasn't more damage. You know what we went through after Heather Creek flooded last spring. You were kind enough to let Frank and me stay here a few days when our house was under water."

"We were happy to help."

"Well, now it's your turn to receive instead of give." Hannah looked pensive. "Fire or flood, they're both so devastating. People often don't even realize how much their home means to them until they face the prospect of losing it."

The Carters had been able to salvage their house after the floodwaters receded, but Charlotte knew there was no hope for Pete's apartment. Bob had told her the burned-out building was a hazard and would have to come down as soon as possible.

"On the other hand," Hannah continued, "Pete's young and sometimes events like this have a way of opening doors we didn't even know were there."

"Or opening our eyes to how much people care about us."

"Or how many good cooks we have right here in Adams County," Hannah teased, sneaking a bite of the chocolate cheesecake that had just been delivered by Mary Louise Henner. "Really, Charlotte, you have to try this. It's delicious."

As Charlotte indulged in a generous forkful of the rich dessert, there was another tap on the door. Then it opened to reveal Melody holding a big pot in her hands with Ashley standing behind her.

Melody grinned. "Can we come in or are you getting tired of all this company?"

"Never tired enough to turn you away," Charlotte assured her as Melody set the pot on the table.

"I made a batch of my secret-recipe pumpkin soup for you. It freezes well, so you can either eat it in the next few days or save it for later."

Charlotte opened the lid to take a peek inside. "It looks and smells delicious."

"It sure does," Hannah agreed. "Is there any way we can convince you to share that secret recipe?"

Melody chuckled. "Not a chance, but if you come into Mel's Place sometime, I'll give you and Frank each a complimentary bowl."

"Sounds good to me," Hannah replied. "Now who wants a glass of raspberry tea?"

"I'll take one," Charlotte replied.

Melody raised her hand. "Me too."

Hannah looked over at Ashley. "How about you, sweetie? Can I get you something to drink?"

"No, thank you," Ashley replied, looking over at Charlotte. "Is Emily here?"

"She's upstairs in her room, I believe. You can go on up and see her if you want."

Ashley hesitated, indecision flashing over her face. "Do you think she'll want to see me?"

"I know she will," Charlotte replied. Then she grabbed the plate of butterscotch bars off the table, hoping they could serve as a peace offering for the girls. "Can you take these up with you?"

"Sure," Ashley said, looking relieved to have an excuse to go upstairs.

After Ashley left the kitchen, Melody turned to the two other women. "She couldn't wait to come out here today to see Emily."

"I know Emily will be happy to see her," Charlotte said, hoping the two girls would find a way to iron out their problems.

"Looks like I might be here for a while," Melody said, shrugging out of her coat. "Is there anything I can do to help?"

"You can help us make room for all of this food," Hannah said, carrying the chocolate cheesecake over to the table along with three forks. "Okay, girls, let's dig in."

EMILY SAT ON THE FLOOR of her room, looking at the remnants of fabric left over from making Pete's sofa pillows and trying to figure out what to do with them.

She, Sam, and Christopher had just finished up a marathon game of Monopoly, and the boys had gone downstairs to play a computer game, giving Emily some time alone.

"Can I come in?"

She looked up, shocked to see Ashley standing in the doorway. "What are you doing here?"

Ashley held out the plate. "I brought you some butterscotch bars."

Emily looked down at the plate and saw only one bar on the plate, along with a bunch of crumbs.

"There were more," Ashley explained awkwardly. "But I passed your brothers in the hallway, and now this is all that's left."

"Thanks," she said, taking the plate from her and setting it on the dresser. She hated this wall of cold politeness between them.

Tears sprang into Ashley's eyes. "The real reason I'm here is that I'm hoping you'll be my friend again even though I've been a complete jerk."

"I'm the one who's been the jerk," Emily replied, rushing over to Ashley. "I never meant any of those things I said about you and Ryan. I was just . . ."

"I know," Ashley interjected. "Me too. When I heard about the fire I realized you could have died without us making up."

"I wasn't in any danger. I stayed up here playing Barbies with Jennifer and Madison during the whole thing." Emily breathed a happy sigh. "But I'm glad you were worried. It means you still want to be my friend."

"Best friend," Ashley said. "Forever and always."

"Forever and always."

The two girls hugged each other, and then Emily picked up the lone butterscotch bar and split it down the middle, handing half of it to Ashley.

"Do you want to come over to my house this afternoon and watch a movie?" Ashley asked her. "I promise not to talk about Ryan the whole time." She grinned sheepishly. "I really like him."

"You can talk about him as much as you want," Emily said, determined to be a better friend from now on. "And I'd love to come over, but I have something I need to do first."

HUNTER WAS IN THE CORRAL with Rambo when Sam dropped Emily off on the road in front of his house. She hadn't called before coming, afraid he'd make some excuse to avoid her just like he'd been doing in school for the last week.

"You sure you don't want me to wait?" Sam asked her, the car idling.

"I'm sure."

She waited until her brother took off again. Then she headed toward the barn, her stomach tied up in nervous knots. After the way she'd treated Hunter, Emily had no idea how he'd react to seeing her now.

As she walked down the long gravel driveway, Emily couldn't tell if Hunter had seen her yet or not. If he had, he was completely ignoring her, focusing all his attention on Rambo as he tossed a saddle blanket over the horse's back.

The closer she got to the corral, the more she doubted the wisdom in coming here. She was so tempted to turn around, but she kept moving forward, determined to say what she'd come here to say.

The horse noticed her before Hunter did, whinnying as Emily walked up to the corral fence and hooked both arms around the top rail.

"Hey, Hunter."

He turned around to face her, two spots of red in his cheeks. "Hey, Emily."

She watched him place the saddle on Rambo and cinch it tight. Since it looked as if he was about to go for a ride, Emily knew it was now or never.

"I just wanted to come over here today to tell you how sorry I am for the way I treated you. I wasn't a very good friend, and I wouldn't blame you if you never wanted to speak to me again."

Hunter walked over to the fence. "Are you crazy? Of course I want to be your friend."

"But when I called the other day, your brother said you were washing your hair."

Hunter looked down on the ground and kicked a pebble with his cowboy boot. "Okay, so I was mad for a little while, but I'm over it."

"Then why have you been avoiding me?"

He met her gaze. "To give you some space. I know I come on a little strong sometimes. I was afraid I'd scared you off by calling all the time and bugging you to go riding."

Emily knew she needed to come clean. "That was partially my fault. I'd been flirting with you and acting like I wanted you to be my boyfriend." She took a deep breath.

"The truth is that I really like you, but just as a friend." She saw a flicker of disappointment cross his face. "Is that okay?"

"Yeah," he replied, his face clearing as he thought about it. "In fact, I like knowing where I stand. Makes life a lot easier since I'm not very good at figuring girls out."

Emily could imagine how confused Hunter must have been when she kept sending him mixed signals. She was also amazed that he'd forgiven her so easily. He had done the same thing back in the summer when she missed his barrel race at the county fair. If she'd been in his shoes, she wasn't so sure she would have been as understanding.

Maybe that had been her problem all along.

Emily had worried too much about her own feelings and not what Hunter and Ashley had been going through.

She put herself in Ashley shoes, trying to imagine how she'd feel if a boy she liked suddenly wanted to date her. Excited, for sure, but nervous too, and worried that she'd blow it somehow. She'd definitely want to talk to her best friend about it.

Hunter placed the bridle on Rambo. "I heard you had a fire at your farm yesterday. We drove by it on the way to church this morning."

"It was pretty messed up," Emily said. "In fact, I should probably get back home."

He mounted the horse and held out his hand. "Need a lift?"

She laughed as she opened the fence to let Rambo out, then she closed it again before climbing onto the saddle behind Hunter.

"Just promise me one thing," Hunter said as he steered the horse toward the road.

"What's that?"

"Let me know if you ever decide you want to be more than friends," he said evenly.

"I will."

She liked this new honesty between them. "Now promise me that we can go riding together over Thanksgiving break, because I've been working with Princess and I think she can beat Rambo in a race."

He laughed. "You're dreaming, Em. Princess wouldn't stand a chance."

"Meet me at the meadow on Friday, and we'll see who's got the fastest horse," she challenged.

"You're on!"

Chapter Twenty-Seven

"The boy needs to be punished."

Charlotte and Bob sat at the kitchen table on Monday morning while a light flurry of snow fell outside. It melted as soon as it hit the ground, but it was a sure sign that winter was coming.

"We don't even know for sure if he's responsible for the fire," Charlotte protested. "Besides, you've seen how Christopher's been acting since Saturday. He's punishing himself enough for what happened."

Bob peeled off the pink paper wrapper from one of the sugar-free bran muffins Nancy Evans had brought over the night before. "That's not the point. Even if there hadn't been a fire, Christopher was doing something dangerous out in the tractor shed and he's old enough to know better."

Charlotte swallowed a sigh. "He was doing it for a school project. You know how he gets caught up in doing a good job."

But Bob wasn't moved by Christopher's good intentions. "That doesn't change the fact that he was setting off sparks in the shed. If we let this go, then what kind of example is that for him? Kids need boundaries, especially eleven-year-old boys."

Deep down, she knew he was right. Kids did need boundaries and structure in their lives. The trick was knowing when to exercise compassion and when to lay down the law.

"Can we at least wait to make a decision about any punishment until we get the report from the fire marshal?" Charlotte asked him, aware that the investigation was happening at that very moment.

The fire marshal had arrived at the farm about an hour earlier, and Pete was out at the tractor shed with him now. Bob had considered joining them but chose instead to let Pete handle it.

Still, by the way Bob was tapping his foot against the floor, Charlotte could tell he was as nervous about the investigation as she was.

"What do you think will happen?" she said, voicing her worst fear. "If it turns out Christopher is responsible for starting the fire, will the insurance company still pay?"

"Yeah, Pete told me he called and checked with the insurance agent. As long as the fire wasn't set deliberately, then we're covered."

She breathed a sigh of relief. "Well, that's good to know. At least we'll be able to put up a new tractor shed."

"But it will have to be smaller," Bob said. "We checked the prices of some prefabricated sheds online. Prices have really gone up in the last year or so. We'll be able to build one just big enough for the tractor to fit inside and little else."

"So no room to set up another apartment."

"Nope," he said, before taking a bite out of his muffin.

Charlotte had been hoping they could find some way to fashion another apartment for Pete in the new tractor shed. Now that idea seemed to be out of the question.

"These are pretty good," Bob said, taking another bite of his muffin. "You should try one."

Charlotte decided to pass. Even though they were sugar-free, she had a lot of calories to work off after eating almost a third of that chocolate cheesecake yesterday. That had definitely not been sugar-free, but it had been delicious.

The door opened, and Pete walked inside the house, tiny snowflakes sprinkled over his dark hair. "It's not too bad outside today. The fire marshal said it's supposed to warm up even more this afternoon, maybe even as high as forty-five degrees."

"What else did he say?" Charlotte asked. "Does he know how the fire started? Was it caused by Christopher's lightning rod?"

"He didn't mention much about the investigation." Pete poured himself a cup of coffee, grabbed a bran muffin, and sat down at the table. "He did find Christopher's makeshift lightning rod in the rubble, though, as well as two flashlight batteries."

"What did he say about that?"

One corner of Pete's mouth turned up in a smile. "He said the lightning rod looked pretty good, considering it was made by an eleven-year-old boy."

Bob turned to Charlotte. "That's why we need to punish him. He's just too smart and creative for his own good. Who knows what half-baked scheme he'll think up next if we don't rein him in?"

"He is a smart kid," Pete agreed. "I wasn't half as smart as Christopher is and I got into trouble all the time."

"You were a handful," Charlotte mused, remembering how many rules she'd set for her kids growing up. Bill never seemed to have any trouble following them, but Pete and Denise had been a different story.

That's why she wasn't sure which way to go with Christopher now. Looking back, she thought she'd been too strict, too inflexible. But how do you find a happy medium?

Pete wolfed down the bran muffin and brushed the crumbs off his hands. "I'm going to head up to Harding today and buy some clothes."

Brad Weber and his buddies had pooled their money to buy Pete a gift certificate at the biggest department store in Harding.

"Need some company?" Bob asked. "We could check out some of the prefabricated buildings up there and see if we find something we like for replacing the tractor shed."

"Might as well." Pete got up from the table. "I don't have anything else to do."

That undercurrent of sadness in Pete's voice bothered Charlotte. He'd had big plans to work on the apartment renovations this winter and now he seemed to be floundering.

After they left, she turned to God for help and comfort. "Heavenly Father," she prayed out loud, her hands folded together on her lap, "please lift the heavy burdens from Pete's heart and give him hope. Heal his pain and give him the strength to move forward. Amen."

GIVING THANKS | 229

THE FIELD TRIP to the city mission in Harding was much better than Christopher could have imagined. He'd certainly never expected to have fun.

"That was cool," Justin Taylor told him as they headed back to the school bus.

Justin, the biggest bully in sixth grade, was actually talking to him.

"Yeah, it was." Christopher was certain this uneasy truce between them wouldn't last. As soon as Justin got mad about something, he'd push Christopher into a locker or call him a name on the playground, but he decided to enjoy it while it lasted.

"One guy gave me this neat marble just for serving him soup. He said it's called a tiger's eye." Justin pocketed his new treasure. "I should come here and volunteer every week. I'd probably really pull in the loot."

Christopher slowed his step to let Justin walk ahead of him. He didn't want to take the chance that they'd end up in the same bus seat together. Justin might be acting nice enough now, but halfway back to Bedford things could go horribly wrong. Then Christopher would be stuck.

When Christopher finally boarded the bus, he realized he'd slowed down a little too much. Dylan and Wyatt were already there and sharing a seat, leaving him to find one on his own.

Unfortunately, there was only one seat left on the crowded bus—right next to Rachel Wells.

Christopher hesitated, frantically looking around for someone to trade seats with him. He knew none of the boys would volunteer to sit with her. That left the girls.

He looked around the bus for Liza Cummings, thinking she might agree to it, even though she'd probably call him a nerd. Then he remembered that Liza had taken off from school two days early because her family was driving down to Texas to spend Thanksgiving with her grandparents.

"Christopher, please sit down," Miss Luka instructed him as the bus driver revved the engine. "We need to get going."

Seeing no other alternative, Christopher slid into the seat next to Rachel. He didn't look at her and sat as far away from her as possible, balancing right on the very edge of the padded seat.

The bus pulled out of the parking lot, and the kids around him all started chattering to each other. All except Christopher and Rachel.

He snuck a glance at her and saw that she was staring straight out the window, trying to ignore him too.

Miss Luka turned around in her seat, which was directly behind the bus driver. "Everyone needs to quiet down. You're getting much too loud."

When nobody seemed to hear her over the noise she clapped her hands together several times until the bus fell silent.

"That's better," she said. "Now, I want to give you a short assignment."

That announcement made everyone groan until she held her hand up to elicit quiet once more. "It won't be hard," she promised. "I want you each to ask your seat partner what they liked best about our visit to the city mission today. Then I want you to write one paragraph about his or her answer in your journal."

Christopher heard Rachel mutter something beside him,

but he couldn't make out the words. He almost wished he'd sat with Justin Taylor instead.

"Okay, let's get this over with," Rachel said as she turned to face him. "Do you want me to go first or you?"

"You can go first," he replied, fearing he might say the wrong thing to her again. He rubbed his stomach, remembering how that had turned out the last time. She hit really hard for a girl.

"All right," she said with a sigh. "The thing I liked best today was helping the cook in the kitchen. She was volunteering today too. She's a teacher for the culinary program at Harding State."

Christopher wasn't sure he heard her correctly and had to get it right for his assignment. "Did you say a *culinary* program?"

"Yep. I'd never heard of it either. The cook told me it's a fancy name for a cooking school. Anyway, she showed me how to make these really cool radish roses and then she let me help her make a salad with some dandelion weeds in it."

"My mom used to make salads like that back in California," Christopher said. "She'd put all kinds of weird-looking stuff in them, like dandelion weeds and flower petals."

"What kind of flower petals?"

"I think they were violets, but you'd better check for sure before you start eating them."

Rachel looked intrigued by the idea of eating flowers. Then she seemed to remember who she was talking to. "Okay, now it's your turn."

Christopher had to think about it for a moment, not sure which part of the day he'd liked the best. They'd played games with the little kids in the morning. Then they helped dish out food for lunch. This afternoon they'd painted a dormitory room in the new building addition. The director of the city mission had told them they had to make the place bigger because they were getting more and more people all the time.

"My favorite part was meeting the people there," he said at last. "I thought it would be kind of scary, but they're just like everybody else. This one kid said they'd been living at the mission because their house burned down and they didn't have anywhere else to go."

Rachel swung her leg back and forth, kicking the seat in front of her. "Bad things happen to a lot of people."

"I know." He thought about Pete losing his home and coming to stay in the spare room. "We had a fire at our farm on Saturday."

"You did?"

He nodded. "If our house had burned down, we might have had to come to live at the mission too."

Rachel looked at him. "You know, you're not as horrible as most boys."

"You said I was a nerd."

"No," she corrected him, "*Liza* said you were a nerd, but she says that to everybody, even me when she gets mad enough. I don't think you're a nerd."

"You don't?" he asked incredulously.

"No, you're okay," Rachel replied. Then she blushed when she saw him staring at her. "But that doesn't mean I like you."

He grinned. "I don't like you either."

Chapter Twenty-Eight

Charlotte toted her two pie carriers up to the front door of the Bedford Gardens Convalescent Center on the Wednesday before Thanksgiving. Connie Krugman, one of the aides at the home, rushed to open the door for her.

"Thank you, Connie," Charlotte exclaimed, ducking inside. "Winter is definitely in the air today."

"That's what I'm afraid of." Connie peered out the window at the gray sky. "My sister is supposed to be driving here from Omaha tomorrow for Thanksgiving. I hope the weather holds so she can make it."

"I hope it does too." Charlotte set down the pie carriers and opened one up. "I come bearing gifts."

Connie peered into the carrier and then her face broke into a wide smile. "You must be the pie lady! Anita's been talking about you—said you promised to bring her a apple-caramel pie for Thanksgiving."

"I sure did," Charlotte acknowledged. "I'm glad she remembered."

"I'm glad you came through for her," Connie said. "So many folks make promises to our residents when they come to visit, and then forget about them after they leave. These pies will brighten everyone's day."

"Would you mind taking these to the kitchen for me?" Charlotte asked. "I'll let the cook decide how she wants to divvy them up among the residents and staff. The two pies on the bottom shelf of each carrier are a special sugar-free version of my cherry-berry pie for the diabetic residents."

"How wonderful." Connie picked up the carriers. "My mouth is watering already."

"Oh, wait a minute," Charlotte said, stepping in front of her. "I need to take out Anita's pie. I'd like to deliver that one to her in person."

"She's in her room," Connie told her. "I'm sure she'll be thrilled to see you."

Charlotte carried the pie down the wing toward Anita's room. The door was open, and she could see her old friend sitting in a chair by the window, a worn Bible open on her lap.

"Hello," she called out. "Am I interrupting?"

"Heavens, no," Anita replied, grinning when she saw Charlotte. "Is that my pie?"

"It sure is." She walked into the room and set the pie down on the table next to Anita. "Do you want to try a bite?"

Anita shook her head. "I think I just want to look at it a while. There are so many beautiful things in life that we take for granted. White lace curtains fluttering in an open window. A tadpole peeking out of a mud puddle. The flaky golden pastry of a fresh-baked pie. The older I get, the more lovely things I see all around me."

Charlotte breathed a contented sigh. "I want to be just like you when I grow up."

Anita chuckled. "You're fine just the way you are. And you're such a joy to all of us here. We're going to enjoy every bite of these pies."

"I'm so glad."

"Me too." Then she reached out to squeeze her hand. "This year, I'm thanking God for the blessing of you."

Tears pricked her eyes at Anita's words. She reached out to hug her. "You are a sweetie."

"Oh, I've still got some vinegar in me yet," Anita teased. "Just wait until I whip everybody at bingo tonight."

Her words made Charlotte laugh, and she suddenly realized how much volunteering at Bedford Gardens meant to her. She might bring gifts like home-baked pies occasionally, but the residents here always gave her so much more.

THAT EVENING AFTER SUPPER, Bob, Charlotte, and the kids gathered around the kitchen table for their evening Bible story.

"Tomorrow is Thanksgiving, and we had a fruitful harvest this year," Bob told the children as he opened the Bible in front of him, "so I chose a passage about the importance of sharing God's blessings with others."

"Like we did for the Adams County Food Pantry?" Christopher asked. "And with the people at the Harding City Mission?"

Charlotte was so proud of how much he'd learned this past month about helping others. He'd told her all about his experiences at the city mission and had even asked if he could volunteer there again soon. She thought it sounded like an excellent idea for the whole family.

"That's right," Bob told him, turning the pages to find the right chapter.

Charlotte cleared the last plate off the table and sat down across from Bob, ready to enjoy some peaceful contemplation before she had to start preparing tomorrow's Thanksgiving feast.

Pete had left for Brad Weber's place right after supper to watch a football game, but not before promising Charlotte that he'd stop by Herko's Grocery Store to pick up some cranberries. She'd forgotten them on her shopping trip yesterday, and they were a necessity for her traditional cranberry salad.

Unfortunately, Pete wouldn't be home until after the game ended, which meant she'd either have to stay up late to make the salad or get up early in the morning so it would have time to set by dinner.

"This reading is from the book of Second Corinthians," Bob told them, sliding his index finger down the page until he found the right spot. "Chapter nine, verses six through eight."

Charlotte pushed away thoughts of her dinner menu and listened to Bob. His evening Bible readings and stories always helped her to focus on the important things in life instead of letting trivial worries, like when to make the cranberry salad, clutter her mind.

Bob cleared his throat then began to read: "Remember this: Whoever sows sparingly will also reap sparingly, and whoever sows generously will also reap generously. Each man should give what he has decided in his heart to give, not reluctantly or under compulsion, for God loves a cheerful giver. And God is able to make all grace abound to you, so that in all things at all times, having all that you need, you will abound in every good work."

"What are sowing and reaping?" Christopher asked. "Does it mean like sewing on a sewing machine?"

Bob peered at him over his bifocals. "It means to plant. We sow corn and wheat and soybeans in the field." He slid the Bible across the table so Christopher could see the words for himself. "And the word *reap* means to harvest. So these Bible verses are talking about planting and harvesting and how important it is to cheerfully give to other people if God has blessed you with a good crop."

Christopher read the verse, his lips moving silently. Then he gave a short nod. "Okay, I get it."

Bob often used a story Bible for the readings, since it was easier for the kids, especially Christopher, to understand. She was about to suggest that he get it when the back door opened and Pete walked inside.

"Is the football game over already?" Sam asked, looking as surprised to see him as everyone else at the table.

"No," Pete said, setting Charlotte's cranberries on the counter. "I left in the middle of the first quarter."

"How come?" Charlotte asked, growing a little concerned. "Has something happened?"

"Brad saw the fire marshal at AA Tractor Supply this afternoon and heard the report was finished. When he told me about it, I figured we'd waited long enough, so I decided to contact the marshal to find out if he'd give us the results of his investigation."

"And . . . ?" Charlotte asked.

"He agreed." Pete reached into his pocket and pulled out a folded piece of paper. "I gave him the number for Brad's fax machine so we could get the report right away. I thought you'd all like to hear what it says, so I came right home."

Christopher paled as Pete unfolded the paper and began to read the report: "An investigation was conducted at Heather Creek Farm, located in Adams County, Nebraska, at the residence of Mr. Peter Stevenson. There is conclusive evidence that the fire was caused by an electrical wiring malfunction in the seventy-year-old building."

Everyone stared at Pete for a moment. Then Christopher looked around the table. "What does that mean?'

Sam turned to him, a wide grin on his face. "It means the fire wasn't your fault."

Christopher's mouth dropped open in shock. "I didn't start the fire?"

"Nope," Pete said, setting the fire marshal's report on the table. "And my paint rags didn't cause it either. If the tractor shed had faulty wiring, we're probably lucky it didn't burn down years ago."

Charlotte thought about Ma Mildred living there, and then about Pete moving in and his plans to set up housekeeping there with Dana after their marriage. She realized now how blessed they were that the fire had happened when the building was empty.

Christopher picked up the report as if he still didn't quite believe it. "Can I keep this?"

Pete shrugged. "I might need it for insurance, but I'll give you a copy."

Bob looked at Christopher. "I'm glad you're innocent of starting the fire, but that doesn't change the fact that you did something wrong."

Christopher met his grandfather's gaze straight on. "I know."

Everyone got very quiet, waiting to hear what Christopher's punishment would be.

Finally Bob said, "Why don't you tell us what you think you did wrong?"

Christopher licked his dry lips. "I made sparks with the batteries in the tractor shed."

"Where should you make sparks?" Bob asked him.

"Outside."

"Wrong answer," Bob told him. "You shouldn't be making sparks anywhere or playing with fire, especially on a farm where there are gas and diesel tanks and all kinds of things that can burn up in an instant."

"Oh."

"Are we clear on that?" Bob asked, his tone serious.

Christopher gave an emphatic nod. "We're clear."

"Okay, then. I'm going to give you some extra chores this week to help you remember."

Relief washed over Christopher's face. "I won't do anything like that again, Grandpa. I promise."

"Whew," Pete joked, breaking the tension. "Dad's rules can be pretty rough. Glad I don't have to follow them anymore."

As everyone started to get up from the table, Charlotte held up her hands. "Hold on. Everybody sit right back down. There's one more thing we need to talk about."

"What?" Sam asked.

"A fire plan." Charlotte had been kicking herself that they hadn't done one before now. The news that the fire was caused by faulty wiring reminded her that you never know when a fire could happen, and she wanted them to be prepared.

"We need to make an escape plan for each bedroom," Charlotte said, "especially on the second floor. We might even have to buy rope ladders to hang out the window in an emergency."

"That would be so cool," Sam said.

"It sure would." Pete grinned. "Especially if you wanted to sneak out at night. I might stay in the spare bedroom permanently if we get to have rope ladders."

Charlotte didn't intend to let them derail her from this discussion. "We'll talk about rope ladders later. The point is, I want us to have a plan in case of an emergency, including a meet-up point so we're not running all over the farm looking for each other in the event of a fire or a tornado."

Pete nodded, growing more serious now. "That actually is a good idea, Mom. When I drove the combine into the yard and saw that the tractor shed was on fire, I was afraid somebody might be in there."

"All right, then," she said, looking at her grandkids. "You three are in charge of writing up a fire plan for us during Thanksgiving break."

"It should be pretty easy," Sam said. "I bet we can find a lot of fire-escape plans on the internet, and then we can customize them to fit the farm."

"I'm glad that's taken care of." Pete rose to his feet. "I'd better get back to Brad's place if I want to see the rest of that football game." He headed toward the door. "Don't wait up for me."

"Curfew is midnight," Bob called after him. "That's the rule everybody staying in this house has to follow."

Pete stopped in his tracks and slowly turned around. "What? Dad, I'm thirty-four years old and . . ."

"Just kidding," Bob said dryly, causing everyone but Pete to burst out laughing.

"You should have seen your face," Sam said, collapsing into another fit of laughter.

Pete smiled and ruefully shook his head as he walked out the door. "You got me, Dad. You got me good."

Chapter Twenty-Nine

The next day, Charlotte opened the oven door, releasing the savory aroma of roasting turkey into the air. She could hear laughter coming from the family room, where Grandma Maxie was entertaining everyone with funny stories and jokes.

Dana and her grandmother had arrived about midmorning, with Grandma Maxie bringing a batch of apricot kolaches still warm from the oven.

Charlotte glanced up at the clock, figuring the meal would be ready in about twenty minutes. That was also the time she expected Chuck and Bonnie Simons to arrive. As she closed the oven door, she heard footsteps behind her and turned around to see Dana standing in the kitchen.

"Is there anything I can do to help? I feel so lazy just sitting around when you're doing all this work."

"You can help me finish setting the table," Charlotte said, handing her some napkins. "I think we'll be able to fit everyone around it without putting the extra leaf in this year."

She felt a pang of disappointment that Bill and his family wouldn't be with them, but she knew it couldn't be helped. A healthy baby was more important than anything else.

"Just think," Dana said, as she laid a folded napkin next to each plate, "next year at Thanksgiving, Pete and I will be married."

"I know." She smiled at her future daughter-in-law. "That's one of the things I'm most thankful for this year."

"Me too."

Pete wandered into the kitchen. "What's going on in here? Do you need a taste tester for the turkey? If so, I'm willing to volunteer."

"Good try, mister," Dana said, "but you have to wait to eat just like everybody else."

When Charlotte finally took the turkey out of the oven, it didn't take long for the aroma to draw the rest of the family into the kitchen.

"Is it time to eat yet?" Christopher asked.

"Not yet," Charlotte told him. "The turkey needs to rest for a few minutes."

"I know what we can do while we wait," Emily said. Then she turned around and ran upstairs. She was back a moment later holding a large gift sack in her hand.

"What's that?" Pete asked her.

"Don't be so impatient, young man," Grandma Maxie chided him, "or I'll have to feed you another one of my kolaches to keep you quiet."

Pete grinned as he turned to his parents. "Now, that's the type of punishment that's *really* effective."

Emily looked up at her uncle. "I know you didn't get to show Dana her Christmas present before the fire..."

"What?" Dana asked, glancing up at Pete. "What Christmas present?"

Pete heaved a long sigh as he turned to face her. "It was lost in the fire. I didn't tell you about it because I didn't want you to be disappointed."

Dana stepped closer to him, laying one hand on his arm. "Oh, Pete, after everything that happened, the *only* thing I want for Christmas is *you*. I thank God you weren't in that tractor shed when it caught fire."

"But a lot of my savings were in there," he confessed. "I was renovating the place for you as a Christmas surprise."

Her face softened. "You were?"

He nodded. "I just wish you'd had a chance to see it before it all went up in smoke."

"Actually," Emily interjected, pulling an envelope out of the bag. "She can see it. I took pictures."

Charlotte stared at her granddaughter in surprise. "When did you do that?"

Emily smiled. "On one of those days when I was moping around with nothing to do. I decided to make designer curtains for Uncle's Pete's apartment, so I took pictures of all the rooms in his apartment to help me come up with the perfect window-covering design. I got everything, the wall colors, the kitchen cupboards, the new furniture..."

"You mean, I can see it?" Dana breathed.

Emily handed her the envelope. "Merry Christmas from Uncle Pete."

No one said a word as Dana opened the envelope and pulled out the stack of photos inside. Tears filled her eyes as she slowly savored each one.

"They're absolutely beautiful," she whispered. Then she looked up at Pete. "I hardly recognize the place. You did so much work."

"I just wanted to make you happy," Pete told her.

She smiled up at him. "You have. Happier than you'll ever know."

"Okay, before it gets too sappy in here, you're not done opening presents." Emily handed over the large gift bag. "I have something else for you too."

Dana opened the bag and pulled out a pair of sofa pillows. "These are beautiful," she said, smoothing one hand over the fabric. "I love the colors."

"They're the same colors Uncle Pete picked out to paint his apartment," Emily told her. "I thought you might like them for your new home, wherever that might be."

Dana turned to him. "You picked those colors out by yourself?"

"You don't have to sound so surprised," he said with a grin. "I might have had a little help from the saleswoman, but I do have good taste."

"That's true," Grandma Maxie chimed in. "Pete has excellent taste. He picked my granddaughter, didn't he?"

They all laughed, even Pete.

"Okay," Pete said, leaning closer to Dana, "so I got lucky picking colors that you liked, just like I got lucky picking my bride."

"Yuck," Christopher said, screwing up his face. "You two aren't going to kiss, are you?"

Pete grinned at him. "I guess we can save it for later."

A knock sounded on the door. "That must be Chuck and Bonnie," Charlotte said, hurrying over to answer it. But when she opened the door, she found Bill and the girls standing on the other side.

"Surprise!" Bill said with a wide smile. "I hope you have room for three more at the table."

Charlotte couldn't believe her eyes. "What are you doing here? And where's Anna? Is she all right?"

"She's fine and she's looking forward to a restful afternoon in River Bend. We're planning to have a small Thanksgiving supper with her parents later this evening, so she suggested that the girls and I spend the day at Heather Creek Farm with all of you."

Jennifer wrapped her arms around Charlotte's knees for a kid-sized hug. "Hi, Grandma."

"Hello there, cutie," she said bending down to kiss the top of her head. "I'm so glad you and your sister and your dad are here." She reached out to embrace Madison. "It looks like we get to put that extra table leaf to good use after all."

Thirty minutes later, the family, including Dana's parents, was seated around the table. Charlotte looked around her as they all joined hands to say grace.

She bowed her head, so very thankful for the circle of love that surrounded her. A hymn filled her head as the prayer filled her heart:

> *Give thanks to God, for good is he,*
> *His grace abideth ever;*
> *To him all praise and glory be,*
> *His mercy faileth never.*
> *His wondrous works with praise record,*
> *His grace abideth ever;*
> *The only God, the sovereign Lord,*
> *Whose mercy faileth never.*
> —Arthur S. Sullivan, 1875

About the Author

Kristin Eckhardt is the author of more than fifty books, including twenty-four novels for Guideposts. She has won two national awards for her writing and her first book was made into a television movie. When she isn't writing, Kristin enjoys traveling with her husband and spending time with their grandchildren.

A Note from the Editors

We hope you enjoyed this volume in the Home to Heather Creek series, published by Guideposts. For over seventy-five years, Guideposts, a nonprofit organization, has been driven by a vision of a world filled with hope. We aspire to be the voice of a trusted friend, a friend who makes you feel more hopeful and connected.

By making a purchase from Guideposts, you join our community in touching millions of lives, inspiring them to believe that all things are possible through faith, hope, and prayer. Your continued support allows us to provide uplifting resources to those in need.

Whether through our online communities, websites, apps, or publications, we strive to inspire our audiences, bring them together, and comfort, uplift, entertain, and guide them.

To learn more, please go to guideposts.org.